A GIFT FOR

_____

FROM

_____

ON THIS DATE

_____

D1056235

WHAT READERS ARE SAYING ABOUT *I DON'T WAIT ANYMORE*

"In her book, *I Don't Wait Anymore*, Grace Thornton shares her struggles as she comes to know and love the edgeless God of the universe as the One who is weaving her life, her story, into a beautiful tapestry of His grace, one in which the full picture will not be seen until we reach our home that God has prepared for us. On page after page, Grace has powerfully captured the essence of God's nature as the One who loves us intimately as He reveals Himself through His Word and uses every moment of our lives to draw us closer to Him, if we are willing to run to Him."

— Dr. Jeff Holland, congregational care pastor, Pinelake Church

"Grace redefines the word *wait* and ignites a fire in my heart I was not expecting! She defines waiting in a way that I wasn't expecting and then makes a case for all of us who are living lives with unrealized expectations, plans, goals, and dreams to stop waiting. By the time I was halfway through, I could not wait to see where she was going with her train of thought."

—An Amazon reader

"A must-read! Grace is spreading light through her writing, and her words are full of encouragement. God has brought me closer to Him through this book. We need more books like this! It is an autobiography of my life. Only it isn't. Such an encouragement to find out that others' journeys are so like my own. Thank you!"

—An Amazon reader

"*I Don't Wait Anymore* explores the story that is present in all of us—a story that each of us must identify and experience lest we settle for a limited view of God and what He wants for us. Grace Thornton's ability to weave together her life happenings and personal convictions brings a new voice to Christian literature that deserves a listen."

—AMY BUFKIN, ADVISOR AND WRITER
FOR REACHINGHER.COM

"Powerful message in a friendly-chat-over-tea style! Life on earth leaves much to be desired. Sure, we can fill our lives with great things and fill our days seeking those fleeting moments of happiness, but we were meant for more. I loved this book because it was a great reminder that we aren't going to satiate those desires with an earthly focus. I know this, but sometimes I get caught up in the fine pearls and abandon the one pearl of great value, and I need something to help me refocus on that which truly makes my heart sing."

—AN AMAZON READER

"Speaks right to my heart, as if [the author has] walked a year in my shoes. I feel like Grace is writing every thought on my heart. I've never read a book where it literally feels like I am reading my own journal. This book is so raw and honest about life's disappointments but also so full of hope and encouragement. And we can see and feel God's life for us in a completely different way. I'm not there, but I get where she is going and she has a way of encouraging you that you can get there, whether overnight or for a longer process. We can all live the life full of joy that God has for us."

—AN AMAZON READER

"Every word packs a punch, knocking down every excuse for not diving into who Jesus is and revealing the overwhelming power of His love."

—MARGARET WALSH, EDITOR
OF THE ROPE BLOG

"Beautifully written with a powerful message. Grace Thornton writes beautifully with the soft voice of an encouraging friend. I read this book, along with a few others, after a serious relationship ended. This was by far the most helpful book because many other books were trying to comfort by saying to get back out there and try to find someone else, which was not what I wanted to hear. Grace so beautifully points out that God's dreams may be very different than our own, so instead of trying to fix our broken dreams, we should change our perspective and abandon our dreams for the satisfying life only God can provide. This book provided the revitalizing kick start that I needed to replace my current dry and stagnant relationship with God."

—AN AMAZON READER

"For anyone whose dreams have been dashed. . . . For anyone who has seen dreams and desires die or be postponed, this book will speak very clearly to your heart and surprise you. I won't give away any of the nuggets of revelation. They're too good, but I closed this book a different person than when I opened it. Thankful for Grace for sharing her journey but more so thankful for the grace of God in her life and mine."

—AN AMAZON READER

"What happens when you pray for something good—like a spouse—and he or she never comes along? Answer: someone infinitely better comes along. This is a keenly felt memoir of a young life put 'on hold' but then wonderfully taken hold of."

—BARRY COOPER, AUTHOR OF *CAN I REALLY TRUST THE BIBLE?*

"Grace Thornton's *I Don't Wait Anymore* is definitely a must-read! It's for anyone whose life's expectations didn't quite work out like they thought, which I'm sure every one of us can relate to. Whether it's marrying someone, divorcing that person, driving a certain car, getting that perfect job, or making that certain salary, everyone can relate on some level. It will encourage you to let go of your expectations and plans and look to God, who holds the master plan of your life. Thornton is a brilliant storyteller, and her heartfelt testimony and real-life stories will keep you captivated. I highly recommend it and hope she writes a second book!"

—AN AMAZON READER

"We all face a choice when our dreams die—do we become bitter or do we surrender ourselves to God? Grace Thornton chose the latter and found meaning and fulfillment in surprising places. An enriching and faith-building journey for anyone searching for God."

—AMY BOUCHER PYE, AUTHOR OF *FINDING MYSELF IN BRITAIN*

"Good for growth! If you don't know how to follow God, found your own spiritual walk grown cold, or want to learn how to pursue Him with all your heart, then this book is a great place to start! Grace has a very down-to-earth way of explaining how she discovered God in her life, and she challenges others to find Him the way she did."

—AN AMAZON READER

"There's something about a story that helps truth to sink in. Grace invites us into an intimate journey of faith. Page by page, she leads the reader to the greatness and beauty of the God who is near and sovereign and satisfying. Read and let your roots sink deep into realities that will not only hold you fast when life hurts but will equip you to live for the glory of God!"

—MATT MASON, SENIOR PASTOR OF
THE CHURCH AT BROOK HILLS

"This is an amazing book! This helped me see how to dig deep into God's Word and find Him. He's writing this story, and it will be perfect if I just trust Him!"

—AN AMAZON READER

I DON'T WAIT ANYMORE

grace
thornton

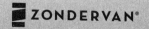

ZONDERVAN®

To all the dear friends and family whose stories have woven through mine over the years. I didn't live this in a vacuum. God has spoken to me over and over and over through your lives, our conversations, our laughter, and our tears. I love you, and I'm blessed to walk this life with you.

CONTENTS

PREFACE

Maybe the most encouraging thing you can hear is this:

Life can feel different. It can be *different.*

Life can be different than it is right now.

I remember what I used to think a good life looked like. I even remember a time years ago when I used to think we all got that kind of life. I had friends who seemed to live it. They loved God, got married, had children, landed good jobs and bought houses, and enjoyed their lives without a lot of complications, without a lot of pain.

And then there was me—there was us, a whole lot of us. And for us life didn't look like that at all.

Things didn't quite work out. Dreams got broken, and it hurt. We found ourselves on a path we didn't want to be on, a path that didn't fit with what we'd always thought was good.

So we felt uneasy about our lives, and we felt uneasy about God. *This isn't what I signed up for. Why did God let my life go this way? Why did my plans not work out even though I felt as though that's what He was calling me to do or to be? Why hasn't He shown up yet like I thought He was supposed to?* And deep in the quiet of our hearts, whether we realized it or not, a wounded whisper grew to a roaring question: *If this is who He is, if this is how He loves me . . . what do I do with that?*

Some of us kept living half-hearted lives, saying we believed what we'd always believed about God, even though our beliefs didn't add up with our reality. Some of us kept walking, hoping everything was still going to work out eventually, albeit a little late. Some of us felt angry with this shocking new version of God that had turned out to be pretty unfair. Some of us walked away from Him.

I can tell you what I did—I tried a lot of things. I tried taking my dreams into my own hands. I tried pursuing new dreams instead. Some of them worked okay. Some of them didn't work at all.

But either way, at the end of the day, the whole thing still didn't sit right in my heart. It didn't feel right. Something felt profoundly wrong, and it wasn't just the fact that life didn't look the way I'd always wanted.

It was bigger than that. I didn't need to find a way to make my life good.

I needed to know what good really was.

I needed that reality to wreck my life, my expectations, my dreams. And I needed it to write a totally different story.

Trying to make my life into something that felt better wasn't going to fix anything. Ever. There was only one thing that would—a new perspective on God and His love for me. I'm not talking about a view that self-talks that "God is in control" to make me feel better. I'm talking about catching a glimpse of who God actually is—not who I thought He was—in such a way that it would wreck me and write new dreams for my life.

I needed to be undone. I didn't need life to be better; I needed it to be radically different.

And maybe, just maybe, it's possible you need the very same thing.

part one

WHAT A GLIMPSE OF A BIG GOD CAN DO

*"You will seek me and find me, when
you seek me with all your heart."*
—JEREMIAH 29:13

one

THE ONE WHO HOLDS MY PATH

I rolled over without opening my eyes, fingers grasping for the alarm. My hand punched through a pyramid of crumpled-up tissues, a perfect pile poised and waiting all night for the perfect breeze to blow it over.

Like my little house of cards. Toppled. I groaned, remembering why they were there. I sank deeper into my bed that morning in Alabama, submerged in a profound emotion I would always remember, the kind that etches itself into your insides. I couldn't resist its force. With eyes squeezed shut, I absorbed deeply the way it sat on my heart, a strange concoction of pain, eeriness, loneliness, and aimlessness. And as the sensation settled, it seared its shocking epiphany on my soul.

Grace, there's a big possibility that your life isn't going to look anything like you thought it would.

The night before, my boyfriend and I had broken up.

We'd been together for a while, since college, and we'd been close friends for years before we ever dated. The loss was big. The death of that relationship sliced deep.

But it wasn't the only thing that died that day. My life plan did too.

And not just because of the breakup. My plans had been limping along for months, and the breakup was the final nail in the coffin. I'd seen a few dream job offers die, as well as a chance to move overseas, and now I had lost the chance at marriage and kids with the guy I thought was meant for me. Up until that point, I'd thought the fulfillment of most of those dreams was pretty standard issue. I'd even thought God had brought me all those things purposefully.

BUT THAT MORNING IT WAS CLEAR SOMETHING
ELSE WAS HAPPENING, SOMETHING SIGNIFICANT.
THE PATH IN FRONT OF ME EVAPORATED, AND THE WHOLE
WORLD BECAME A BLANK SLATE.
FOR THE FIRST TIME.

I'd always had goals or expectations propelling me forward—elementary school led to junior high, which led to high school and then to college. From there, college would naturally give way to a career and marriage and motherhood and grandparenthood.

There was always someplace to go, some reason to put one foot in front of the other, something to be.

Until that morning. That morning I woke up as just Grace—Grace with a naked soul. The sheet that covered me was too thin, the air too thick, the unknown future too gaping a chasm. I shivered as I lay there soaking in my new unwanted reality. This was big. For the first time in my life, my plans had withered to mind-blowing nothingness.

I was naked before God. Stripped of dreams. Nothing on the horizon.

And nothing to do but stand up, get ready, and go to work.

I stood on shaky legs and spun around, dog leash dangling in my hand. From that spot on the hill, England looked the same in every direction. Rolling hills. Grass now brownish-yellow in the autumn sun. Trees and blackberry bushes laden with fruit that no one had picked, because it seemed no one walked this way. Ever.

There was no path anymore.

The golden lab huffed through the field ahead of me, zigzagging through the flaxen knee-high grass. It was difficult to see where she was, and even more difficult to see where she was going.

"Holly. Holly, come!" I yelled in my best British accent—and by best, I mean horrific. I instantly regretted it—I felt it scrape my own eardrums as it bounced back at me. But the dragged-out southern "Hah-lee" that rolled out of my mouth apparently didn't even remotely resemble the lab's name in her mother tongue. She never answered to it.

But my fake brogue didn't do it either.

Holly was nowhere.

We'd been following a well-labeled footpath until it evaporated into hayfields. Past the end of the trail, a few more steps were beaten down in the tall grass, but even those stopped not far from where they began.

It felt like we were all alone. It felt like *I* was all alone.

"Holly! Holly, come!"

For a second I looked back at the path that had pitched us out here and thought about going back the way we'd come, but I quickly dismissed the idea. That kind-eyed lab was somewhere up ahead of me, and even though it looked like this field had escaped foot traffic for years, it was clear Holly had been here before.

I pulled out a tiny whistle I'd tucked in my pocket and blew four quick puffs. Something stirred at the bottom of the hill.

I SAW THE FIELD RIPPLING TOWARD ME, AND SUDDENLY THE WAVES OF GRASS SPIT OUT A SMILING DOG AT MY FEET.

She looked at me and then turned around and ran back in the direction from where she'd come.

She sure seems confident. I tucked the whistle into my pocket.

I guess I'm going to have to trust.

I'll be honest. On the morning following the breakup, when the well-marked path of my growing-up years pitched me out as a crying, broken mess into a field of mangled dreams, trusting God with the blank future felt a lot like setting off warily after that golden lab. I knew Holly was out there somewhere, but I couldn't see her, and I really had no idea if I was going to like where we ended up. But what choice did I have? I went with it. And I was going to go with this too, this whole blank life thing.

I BELIEVED GOD WOULD TAKE CARE OF ME—I REALLY DID. MY FUTURE WAS GOING TO BE FINE. BUT WAS IT GOING TO BE GOOD? I WASN'T SURE.

My heart felt so hollow, and the desire for companionship and direction overwhelmed me. That morning I didn't feel God. I didn't feel the weight of peace I thought was supposed to come when I put my trust in Him. I felt heartbroken, disappointed, and lost.

And I didn't know what to do next.

"Wait, you're where? You're on which side of the train tracks?"

Holly and I bounded up the wooden steps that led over the steep bank of the tracks as my friend Carol—Holly's owner—consulted an old homemade map she'd spread over the kitchen table and shown me that morning before the lab and I left for our way-longer-than-planned jaunt.

Surely it can't be that hard, I remember thinking as I'd studied the drawing. The hand-sketched map depicted age-old property lines, fields linked together with a dotted path snaking right through the middle of them.

I'd taken a picture with my phone and thought I wouldn't even need it. *I'm sure there will be markers, that the path will make sense.*

I was wrong.

I stood on the steep bank near the tracks, pulled the phone from my ear, and looked around. Holly's tongue hung out of the left side of her mouth, the air heavy with the sound of her panting.

"I can see St. John's Church in the distance on the other side," I said finally.

She paused. "Right. I know exactly where you are."

And as Carol gave me a laundry list of directions— "walk through this horse pasture, the horses might come at you but they're really nice," and "walk a little ways through the trees," and finally, "turn back onto the main road at the end of the lane"—the tired dog and I found our way back home.

Holly sniffed my pocket for a treat. I gave her what little I had, knowing she deserved prime rib. She'd done her best, even though I'd resisted a lot of her suggestions— I'd struggled to trust that her idea of the best path didn't have more to do with chasing squirrels than getting home.

Now, back inside the house and full of biscuits, Holly sprawled across the kitchen tile next to the table with the map still spread across it. My eyes traced the pencil-drawn route that had looked so simple hours ago. Having a plan had done me no good when the path disappeared.

What had gotten me through in the end was knowing the person who knew the way home—and knowing her well enough to put my path in her hands with joy and relief.

On that tear-soaked morning in Alabama as I watched my plans melt away into nothingness, I longed to see the map of where all this was headed. I wanted God to roll it out across the kitchen table, explain it, and let me snap a photo that I could keep in my pocket to make sense of things later. But just like that day in England, a map was honestly the last thing I needed.

WHAT I NEEDED WAS TO KNOW THE ONE WHO HELD MY PATH, AND I NEEDED TO KNOW HIM IN A WAY I'D NEVER KNOWN HIM BEFORE.

I needed to know Him *better than anything or anyone else*.

But when I lay there that morning, tissues crumpled in my fist, I really thought I *did* know Him well enough. A whole lot of how I'd spent my life and how I'd made my decisions had involved Him. I'd done all I knew to do to love and worship Him: I loved Him; I trusted Him; and I truly believed that He—the all-powerful God who held my life in His hands—had my best interest at heart.

But as the hurt bounced around in my soul like a ball in a pinball machine, I felt keenly the hollowness where peace should have been. And I felt the hollowness of the words that rolled out of my heart and off my lips, words that should have been chock-full of hope and strength when they're headed toward the God of the universe during the moments of our deepest hurt.

Words like *trust* and *love*.

I knew easily what love meant to me on a human level when I thought about the boyfriend I'd lost the night before. When I was with him, love was light on its feet with the all-consuming feeling of "I'll go anywhere and do anything as long as you come with me." I'd felt that passion reach into the depths of my heart and take hold of me, burning like an out-of-control blaze and incinerating any future plans I'd had. And I was happy to see them go. I'd never been more content.

Life is a big adventure when love takes over like that. Even the toughest moments are washed with a redemptive glow.

But when I thought about God, *love* felt weak and flat, like a faded construction paper sign on a church bulletin board. *Love* meant that I believed in Him, that I knew He had done a whole lot for me, and that I was grateful. It meant that I talked to Him about my life and cared about whether or not He was happy with my choices and decisions.

And when tough times came, I asked Him for help . . . but I also questioned Him like a prosecutor looking for a crack in His character. I always knew His way would win out, but when His plans overruled mine, and what He wanted for me didn't line up with my plans, I'd slink away like a child headed to clean her room *just because He said so*.

That was the love I felt for God, and somehow I thought those two definitions—the all-consuming relationship love and my love for God—were the same.

Wow.

It was like I gave God His own dictionary when it came to the most vibrant words there are, and I assigned those words sterile and formulaic definitions that didn't ring true in my human heart. And I didn't even realize that there was something terribly skewed about that.

So I carried on "loving." Trust lived the same kind of soul-numbing half-life, and that showed on the day I buried my dreams—I trusted God like I'd trust a funeral director to take care of all the arrangements properly. I didn't trust Him like an intimate friend whose arms I could fall into with tear-stained relief because *hallelujah, here's the Person who came just because He knows me and loves me.*

IN THAT MOMENT I NEEDED A GOD I COULD TRUST WITH MY AGONY–RIDDEN, EMOTION–ETCHED HEART, NOT JUST WITH MY LIFE'S STRATEGY.

That's why my "trust" didn't work, didn't flesh itself out in peace and depth of faith. My version of trusting God was just words. It was distant. Impersonal. It made it into my pep talks but not into the depths of my pain. For years my worship had been indifferent, like the occasional commuter's nod to the grandiose mountains on the horizon. I'd never known God up close enough to be wrecked by His love, close enough to want to put my dreams in His hands with joy and relief, close enough to let Him write new dreams if He wanted.

My faith had stayed small, stunted like a plant that sat for years out of the sun's rays but saw them streaming through the windows every day from the other side of the room.

It's hard to trust the intimate details of our lives to a God we don't know intimately.

And it's even harder to find joy in that surrender.

I wish I could tell you that girl with the tissue pile got out of the shadows and into the sun that day. But that'd be a lie. She didn't.

In fact, it was quite a while that I kept living my version of "trusting" God, working and running and biking and making friends and building a life for myself. I tried to make my blank slate productive, to take the mess of broken pieces and build something new on my own. I was pursuing a life with drive. A life with purpose.

And all the while, Someone was pursuing me.

HOW DOES IT FEEL TO KNOW SOMEONE IS PURSUING YOU?

_____
_____
_____
_____
_____
_____
_____
_____
_____
_____
_____
_____
_____
_____
_____
_____
_____
_____
_____
_____

two

WHEN EVERYTHING SEEMS "GOOD ENOUGH"

The cloud of dust that billowed up behind the light-blue Chevy truck rolled forward over the cab each time we slowed to a stop on the brown gravel road that wound along the top of the Mississippi River levee.

All the way to Louisiana, pastureland sloped off to the left and right of the one-lane road, which sat perched right on top of what's got to be the longest man-made hill in the world.

At the bottom of the hill to the west were deer-filled woods that quietly waited for the entire county—including my older brother—to descend upon them come hunting season. The river was back there in the distance, miles away through the trees, but occasionally the water would rise all the way until it licked the grassy slope of the levee, reminding everyone why the big hill needed to be there in the first place. But on the eastern side, there were horses grazing away, living their lives.

AS A NINE-YEAR-OLD GROWING UP IN MISSISSIPPI, THIS WAS MY FAVORITE PLACE IN THE WORLD.

As soon as the truck stopped, I'd open the passenger-side pickup door and hit the crunchy gravel with my to-the-knee, black rubber boots. There are a lot of things I don't remember—or want to remember—about my thought processes as a kid. But there's one thing I do know:

I had a one-track mind. And that track was horses.

Instead of Barbies, I had model horses and ranching families behind the couch in our den. I loved books, but I loved them most if they were about horses or people who rode horses, or if they were that impossible rags-to-riches kind of fiction about preteens who managed to bond with crazy fast horses while stuck on desert islands and then trained them to win national derbies.

At that stage in life, I had dreams that were pretty Triple Crown-centric, dreams that didn't have a prayer of coming true. But I was happy every Saturday when my boots walked me off the gravel road and onto the rolling green slope on the east side of the levee. I had horses to love, and I knew they were going to love me back. Especially one.

Don't get me wrong, I loved them all the same. Dorky, little nine-year-old Grace loved every single horse in the whole wide world the same.

But there was this black one with a gray nose that always saw Dad and me coming and didn't run. The other horses played a lot harder to get—they were skittish and a little wild. Most of the horses left out on the levee to graze were just that—left out on the levee. Not in someone's stable behind the house, not taken out for a weekly ride. They weren't uncared for, but they weren't engaged often, other than to make sure they were still there and okay.

So they understandably didn't grasp the appeal of a kid barreling out there in boots to make friends with them. A few would move around me in a nervous circle, unsure if they wanted to be involved, trying to gauge if Dad and I had something to give them that made it worth the risk. Eventually they would sniff the empty truck bed and then join the rest of the herd that stayed out on the perimeter, unimpressed and uninterested.

But not the little black horse. He always welcomed the overwhelming amount of love I had for him. I'd wrap my arms around him and face-plant into his neck and climb on his back, and he never seemed to mind. In fact, he actually seemed to like it. He'd see me coming and take a couple of steps toward me, almost as if he could smell the love emanating from my little-kid heart. I'd stick out my hand, and he would put his nose in it and huff, like he got me and knew why I was there. That was pure awesomeness in my kid world.

So there's a detail I haven't mentioned yet. That little horse . . . he was a little bit lame. I remember the first time we realized it. Dad ran his hand down the horse's leg and looked at it, but it was difficult for him to tell if the lameness was caused by a temporary injury or if he was permanently gimp-legged. Over time it became clear the limp wasn't going away. That realization sat heavy in my heart, and as we drove away one Saturday, I looked back at the horse, whose head was turned to watch us go.

"Dad, do you think he really wishes he could run away like the others?"

Dad thought for a second, and then he smiled. "Nah, I don't think so. I think the fact that he's a little too lame to run away fast definitely makes him easier to catch. But I also think it makes him love even more the fact that you notice him. I think he's happy to be caught."

Flying through fields fifteen years later, I like to think that you couldn't have caught us if you tried.

We sped down the narrow road through the Alabama state park, thin bike tires humming on the smooth pavement. As we passed a pasture, several horses flicked their ears in our direction. Totally disinterested, they went right back to doing whatever it was they were doing before the herd of girls showed up on the periphery of their stomping grounds. They'd seen enough bicycles to know that we were friend, not foe, and that we weren't coming any closer.

Those days I mostly saw my old four-legged buddies from a distance. But I'm pretty sure they could still see it in my eyes. *Horse girl.* The fondness was still there, but the zeal had definitely cooled over the years. And I'm guessing that's a good thing—the job market is not that awesome these days for cowgirls or too-tall jockeys looking to make champions out of shipwrecked Arabian racehorses. At least that's what I'm told.

But employment opportunities *were* pretty decent at that point for a girl looking for a slightly more normal job to pour her life into. And I did just that. I poured my life into a meaningful job I liked, and I felt God had led me there.

After work hours, I'd hit the pavement with my friends, either on foot or on two wheels.

THE SUMMER DAYS IN ALABAMA STRETCHED LONG LIKE A TIRED GOLDEN LAB ACROSS THE KITCHEN FLOOR, AND IN THE BEST KIND OF WAY.

Often the sun was long set by the time we loaded our bikes back up or walked away from an outdoor café downtown where we'd stopped for dinner after a run.

Life was going fine, and the years ticked by. But there was a nagging, antsy feeling that swelled at night when I lay in bed or during the workday when I'd sip tea, glance out the window, and my soul would get quiet for a second. A deep sensation would creep up behind me, making me feel as though I were sipping tea with my back to the Grand Canyon, heels up against the edge—occasionally my foot would scrape backward a half inch and send a pebble bouncing into the chasm. I couldn't see it, but I could hear and feel its yawning pull behind me. And I knew that hole wanted to swallow me.

There's something missing—I feel it. I assumed it was my dreams, the dreams that still lay in pieces where they'd fallen and shattered on the floor of my rented townhouse. I assumed it was because my life didn't fit what I'd wanted, didn't follow the well-beaten path. People who were barely more than strangers on the street could point to the visible holes in my life, and if some brave person did every now and then, they'd also tell me places I could go to get them filled—church, grad school, online dating, the gym.

So I took it to heart.

I traveled. Lots. I started a master's degree with a vengeance. I quit doughnuts and ran a whole bunch of half marathons. I worked hard. I got more deeply involved in my church. I met up with friends to pray for God to bring us husbands, and then I tried some things to put feet to those prayers—blind dates, different small groups at church, singles events.

When I was busy, I didn't feel the cavernous hunger so much, but with every day that failed to fill it, the void deepened and crept into my tea breaks and sleepless nights.

I was flying ninety-to-nothing on my own steam over the smooth pavement of my twenties, my stomach full enough to get by, my love for God as empty as the bed of my dad's light-blue Chevy, even though big parts of my life revolved around Him and His Church. If I'd been honest with myself, I was living a lot like I'd been let out to pasture, like I felt that God had created my world and then turned me loose to live my life, checking in on me occasionally to make sure I was doing okay.

I definitely didn't picture God's love like the love of a nine-year-old running in boots, busting a gut to get to me just because He cared about me. Just like my love for God was hollow, my definition of His love for me was hollow too. The love I had wrapped my brain around could fill a few minutes of reading my Bible in the morning, but it could've never filled the Grand Canyon. If someone had told me His love could change literally everything, I would've thought, *Of course it can—just like Jesus is always the answer, and we "trust" Him with everything and "love" Him more than anything else.*

I HAD NO IDEA WHAT HIS LOVE REALLY FELT LIKE OR WHAT IT COULD DO, SO I HAD NO IDEA HOW VAST ITS ABILITY TO SATIATE.

I really did feel like the knowledge of His presence and love helped, but it was more like a meal in my diet than the thing that stopped the hunger in its tracks with finality. I attributed the hunger to the "normal life" things that I wanted and didn't have, and I turned to Jesus to provide the things I needed to satiate that hunger.

And though I felt the pangs and was trying hard to quiet them, I had no idea how empty I really was. Or that the cavernous hunger *was really for God Himself*, and that really did mean something bigger than what I'd always thought.

John Piper said the reason we don't feel the depth of the hunger we have for God is because we've nibbled at the table of the world for so long, anesthetizing our desire with lesser things. Lesser dreams. Lesser love. Those lesser things aren't good enough to kill the hunger pangs, but they keep us just full enough that we aren't desperate enough to put our whole lives on the line and seek out the permanent remedy.

Especially if we're told that remedy is God. We feel like we've already been riding that train, and though we may revere it, it's never gone anywhere that hit us on a deep, day-to-day, gut-changing level.

We're doing well enough out here on our own. I mean, there's grass from here to Louisiana to fill our stomachs. We think if we could just get that one thing we wanted, it would quell some of our hunger. We have an endless supply of one more thing to try. Our hunger's manageable, so we feel like God works well as a side item.

WE DON'T EVEN KNOW WHAT WE'RE MISSING BY NOT CRAVING HIM AS THE ONE THING WORTH TRADING EVERYTHING ELSE FOR.

We're conditioned to a world where all good things exist on the same plane—the visible, edible world in front of us that we can see and touch and post on our newsfeeds. We've seen church and God and spirituality touch that world in a way that doesn't match the kind of power-filled words we hear used by the preachers and the Bible, and when we feel the disconnect, often that's when our own dictionary gets written—and goes on the shelf.

And in a world crowded with things that look real enough, our thumbs keep scrolling and our hearts keep roaming around the temporal, looking for the next good thing. If we're honest, this is probably what we will do for the rest of our lives, unless we stand still and stop deadening the pain and filling the space with noise, with stuff to do.

This is where our lameness can become the best gift we've ever received, if we'll stop and let it say what it needs to say to us. It can change our lives, our dreams, for the *better*. If we can stand in that hurt and feel it deeply for what it is— all the deep lacerations, the hollow hunger, the raw scars, and the crevasses filled with salt—it will whisper truth to us. Pain, as C. S. Lewis said, becomes God's megaphone straight into our hearts, because it wakes us up to the fact that some things are just too big to have a solution here on earth.

And in the face of the gaping hunger, insatiable by anything short of the kingdom of heaven filling us up, we have a choice.

We can shake our fists at the One who made us, beat our fists against His chest in anger and bitterness. Or we can let our hurt drive us to desperation for real comfort, our hearts holding up the white flag of surrender in the face of His real love. We'll stand there, knowing nothing we've tried or will ever try will give us the fullness offered by the One who looks us in the eye and sees all the way into the depths of our hearts.

Finally, we won't try to run anymore. We'll pick up our throbbing feet, and we'll take a step toward the One who's come after us.

And when we do, our words will be rewritten.
And our life story will really start to sing.

Looking back on those days in Alabama, it's hard to understand why I spent so many years content to keep at arm's length what I knew in my heart was the only thing that would set things right.

But it's hard to imagine how a hurricane might wreck your heart when all you know of wind is what comes from a lazy, southern ceiling fan.

I didn't take God's love seriously enough. I'd never gotten close enough to taste it. I didn't put in the effort to see if what I'd always heard had something deeper going on than what I had experienced. It's a good thing my dreams got wrecked.

If my dreams had kept being served up one after the other, if everything had kept tasting generally okay, I might never have pushed my chair back from the table, wiped my mouth, and said, "Enough." That deep hunger creeping up behind me might never have gotten my full attention if it hadn't been rubbed raw by the violent death of my plans.

It's hard to see our hurt as a gift. But when we pull back and look at the whole story, the one that lasts billions of years, that's exactly what it is. Because this life dissipates faster than dust kicked up on the levee, and if short-lived hurt quickens our ears to hear the depth of love on the horizon and tunes our hearts to receive it, then we'll rejoice for the rest of eternity for the friendship brought to us by our pain.

It's so counterintuitive. It takes our newsfeed world and turns it on its head.

WE KNOW DEEP IN OUR HEARTS THERE'S A BIGGER STORY AT PLAY HERE, SOMETHING GRAND AND BEAUTIFUL WITH DEEP RISK AND DEEP PAYOFF.

Why else would we constantly be striving for something, aware that there's something better, more fulfilling out there to be had? We know there is more. We're always looking for it. Our hunger speaks to that truth.

And the God who gave us the longing is driving up the road toward us, holding the remedy in His hands.

ARE THERE POINTS IN YOUR DAYS WHEN YOU FEEL A RESTLESSNESS OR HUNGER THREATENING TO OVERTAKE YOUR HEART? WHAT DO YOU NORMALLY DO TO APPEASE THAT RESTLESSNESS? _____

_____

_____

_____

_____

_____

_____

_____

_____

_____

_____

_____

_____

_____

_____

_____

_____

_____

_____

_____

_____

_____

_____

_____

_____

three

WHEN YOU BRUSH UP AGAINST SOMETHING REAL

The early-morning rain was beating steadily against the window, but it didn't drown out the laughter that made it all the way through the door and through the layer of sleep wrapped around my brain.

Cram eight mid-thirties women into an Alabama lake house for the weekend, and it's like we forget who we are in the outside world. We want to stay up all night talking. We think we can run on no sleep like we used to in college.

I groaned and smashed my face back into the pillow. *No. Not enough sleep. Too old for this.*

The day before, all eight of us had been hanging out and telling stories until well after midnight. It was great but exhausting, and I felt like my eyes were crossing by the time I hit the pillow.

"Grace, are you asleep?"

"Almost. But not yet."

I didn't know if my friend Amy H just hadn't hit the wall yet, or if she was still running on a high from the day, but suddenly she was telling me all about the Hubble telescope. She's a middle school science teacher. But still.

"There are more stars in the sky than grains of sand on all the earth's beaches. Grace, did you hear that? *More stars than all the grains of sand on all the earth's beaches.*"

At this point in the evening, I didn't have a prayer of hanging with her in this conversation. I was out like a light, leaving her mid-sentence.

The next morning after I pried my face from my pillow, I faced my shame. I brewed tea, walked out on the back deck facing the lake, and pulled up a chair next to my favorite scientist.

"Okay, Amy," I said. "I'm ready. Hit me."

"Hit you with what?"

"All that Hubble telescope stuff you were trying to tell me about last night. I've had sleep and caffeine now."

Her eyes lit up.

"Well, it's orbiting in space, and it can see billions and billions of galaxies. It has shown that there are more stars than there are grains of sand on all the earth's beaches. The longer it's up there, the farther it can see, and it hasn't even found the edge of the universe yet."

I shook my head.

"It just makes me think about how incredibly big God is," she said. "The fact that He *created* a universe so big we can't even find the edge of it after decades of looking for it. I mean, that's just crazy."

Um, yeah, that *is* crazy. I can't wrap my mind around the idea of *edgeless*. I don't have a box for that.

WHEN I THINK OF WHAT CRAZY BIG LOOKS LIKE, I THINK ABOUT THE OCEAN, SOMETHING I CAN SEE AND STICK MY TOES IN.

And the ocean has pretty comprehendible edges.

Even though I'm overwhelmed with the vastness of the ocean versus my smallness, when I'm standing in those billions of grains of sand and staring out at the water, I know there's another continent somewhere on the other side of it telling it where to stop. Its bigness still has bounds— bounds we can measure, breadth we can jump across in an overnight plane ride. The bigness that Amy talked about was entirely different.

That crazy ridiculous telescope has had its eye sprinting toward the edge of the universe since 1990, looking farther and farther every second for decades, and it still hasn't been able to find an edge. *At all.* That makes the ocean seem like a raindrop. Suddenly, the God who spoke the whole universe into being seems exponentially enormous in a way we don't have the vocabulary to express or the brain cells to comprehend. And just think of it. *We can know Him.*

Our edgeless God—as infinitely perfect as He is big—wrapped Himself in flesh and came here to live among imperfect humans just so we could see how big His love for us really is. Through His Son, Jesus, He brought a bigger-than-the-universe love down in an ocean-size form so we could see Him, walk around Him, dip our toes in who He is. He is perfect, as the Father is perfect. All-knowing. All-powerful. All-loving. All *here.*

We needed to see Him here. And He needed to be here in order to die in our place. The light Jesus brought *here* drives us to look up *there,* to the infinite Father God who sent Him.

WE CAN KNOW HIM, THE GOD WHO HOLDS THE WORLD IN HIS HANDS AND HOLDS OUR TEARS IN A BOTTLE.

He knows the names of every star and every miscarried baby. He tells the oceans where to stop, and He tells me how to get through the day. He knows where each planet will travel, and He knows what will be on my mind when I lay my head on the pillow tonight.

And He *cares*.

Seriously. *Who is like our God? And what love is like His love?*

When our hearts burst with the reality that *this God* is the One who loves us on a deep, personal level, our skin threatens to explode with the sheer outrageousness of the reality sitting in our souls. It's too big to handle. It doesn't fit in our brains or sit well on a pew or on a shelf. And we can't come into contact with it for real and walk away without a totally wrecked heart. That's why in Scripture we see a lot of restless, radical language used to describe the people who really saw God. We see people who lived their lives as foreigners on the earth, wandering with unsettled hearts, longing for something they knew they couldn't find at sea level, putting all their hopes in the world still to come. "Therefore God is not ashamed to be called their God, for he has prepared for them a city" (Hebrews 11:16). We see grown men and women throw down lives and livelihoods, leaving everything behind at the sound of two words: *follow Me*. We see a man named Moses who came down off a mountain with a face glowing so brightly that other people couldn't even look at him, just because God had passed nearby. And God did that because Moses asked Him to, because He and Moses had been friends for years, because He knew Moses and Moses knew Him.

"Please show me your glory" (Exodus 33:18).

Have you ever known anyone who has seen Him, really seen Him? It's unmistakable in the same way a person in love is unmistakable. You can't miss what it does to a human heart, and you can't fabricate it either.

His love, His presence marks a life.

And it glows.

Her name is Sarah.

She has some serious reservations about being compared to Moses. I don't blame her. But the truth is, from day one, I knew there was something really different about her. I met her in college and immediately had questions I didn't even know how to articulate. Questions that would stick with me for years.

She was part of my circle of friends at the small Christian college we attended. We stayed up late doing things like trying to figure out how to climb into the university's clock tower, having water gun wars, and pushing each other downhill on rolling office chairs.

Life was simple. We went to class, and we played. It was a blast. I felt like I'd found my people.

But somewhere in the middle of too little sleep and too much Mountain Dew, we started to go through the throes of morphing from teen to adult. We changed our majors, had regular flip-outs about the future, and talked about marriage all the time. We had the typical breakups, proposals, and love triangles that happen when you have several thousand singles in a square half mile. It was dramatic at times, but we weathered it together. It was normal in a good way, I thought. But then there was Sarah. And Sarah really threw me off.

As we rode the waves of drama, she seemed so unaffected. It was like peace filled her up and radiated from her eyes. I wondered if it was just her personality. I knew she knew God. But . . . so did I. Right? And when the drama came, I was very much affected.

Many mornings in between Tae Bo® and literature class I would sit in my dorm room and read the Bible over a bowl of Reese's Puffs. I knew the Bible was important. I knew God cared for me. I felt Him speak to me through verses I read. I journaled prayers to Him about what was happening in my life, questions I had, the struggle to figure out who I was supposed to be and what I should do. *Oh, the angst.*

WHAT DID GOD WANT FROM ME? WHAT WAS HE DOING WITH ALL THE STUFF GOING ON IN MY LIFE?

Why were some things just not working out? I hashed it out with my buddies. I waited for Him to act, to speak.

And in the midst of it, Sarah would sneak off by herself to a hotel in another town for the weekend to spend time alone reading God's Word and seeking His face. I didn't know any other twenty-one-year-old who did that. I had so many questions.

"While you were there, did you feel like you heard God tell you anything about what to do?"

She didn't.

If that had been me, I would've thought the trip was kind of a bust. Surely if you're going to invest that kind of time alone, God should show up with some answers. But to her, it didn't matter. That wasn't why she went. She just felt like God was calling her out to spend some time with Him, to spend time in His Word. She felt like her soul needed it. The answers were secondary. Her peace never wavered. I didn't get it.

My life was full of Jesus. Lots and lots of Jesus, I thought. But even though I'd grown as a result of my Reese's Puffs routine and girls' Bible study and mentoring, serving, and hanging out with other believers, the way I saw Sarah living was on a whole different plane. I had brushed up against something real. Sarah knew God.

She knew God on a deep, deep level, a level that gave her a noticeable air of calm contentment. She loved life, but life didn't ruffle her—it was secondary. It was like she and God had some sort of inside joke going on, and I didn't get it. She had bad days, sure. She experienced difficult times. But I never saw her universe get rocked, not by her decisions or her job choices or her singleness. It made me sit up and take note, even though I didn't totally understand what I was seeing.

She knew the God of the universe in such a way that she genuinely wanted nothing else. And I didn't. I might've thought I did, but I didn't.

If I had known God the way Sarah did, I doubt I would've faced off with Him in my twenties, pointing at my pile of broken dreams and asking Him to explain Himself.

Why isn't this working out? Why don't You fix it? So many *whys*.

Don't get me wrong. *Why* is okay sometimes. It's a human word that pours from a heart cracked and bleeding, a heart that wakes up every morning in an earthly zip code and can't grasp the universe.

BUT MY *WHY* HAD GROWN TOO LARGE BECAUSE MY GOD WASN'T BIG ENOUGH.

He'd receded into the dusty corners of my room and bookshelves. He'd been brought down to where I thought I could see Him, but not in a good way.

God's Word wasn't magnifying His vastness to my soul

as I got to know Him better and better. Because I had sized Him up already.

He was ocean-size in my heart, not edgeless and unfathomable. Still massive, don't get me wrong. Still big enough to do something about the way my life was going if He wanted to. Big enough to be at fault for the stuff that wasn't going quite right. But not big enough to be trusted or for me to view Him as the Prize life is lived to win.

Because of that, I viewed Him all wrong. I saw Him walking around healing—but healing only the people He chose, and I didn't think that was fair. I saw Him meeting the needs of others differently from how He met mine, and I didn't see justice in it. I saw Him as small enough to point my finger in His face and say He'd done it wrong. Done *me* wrong.

But God never came here in touchable form so that I could feel like His peer. He didn't do it so I could feel like we were intellectual equals working side by side on how the puzzle pieces of my life should fit together. If He had, it would make perfect sense why I would feel stinging hurt at the hand of a God who thinks the same way I do but pulls rank and trumps what I want for "His will," just because He can. If that were true, He would be a God I could wrap my mind around. But that God isn't God at all.

He didn't come for us to wrap our minds around Him; He came to wrap His arms around us, to show us the heart of a Father, to give us a taste of what's to come.

HE BROUGHT HIMSELF HERE SO THAT WE COULD KNOW HIM, NOT HOW TO MANIPULATE THE LIFE WE WANT FROM HIM.

A God I'm able to manipulate misses the infinite reality of a God who has the whole universe in His back pocket. It misses the fact that the reason He made Himself touchable was so that we could know His love, the infinite love of an edgeless God.

It misses the whole point.

And there it was, the deadliest enemy of my heart and soul—a moderately big God. That perspective crippled me for years.

It's no surprise that a little further into my twenties, I found myself still wondering how to bridge the gap between Sarah's peace and my own unanswered questions, my own frustration. The glow I'd seen in her had followed me, etched permanently into my memory, but I couldn't comprehend how sweeping the change would be if I could just see God up close. And I couldn't figure out how to get there from here.

The mountain of dreams I'd built in the pages of my prayer journal had unraveled. I was just living life. And before I knew what was happening, I had no idea where God was in the middle of it. He'd become like drab wallpaper, so ordinary I didn't really notice it anymore, a faded backdrop against which I lived my life every day. I knew He was there, and I thought I knew His ways. But when it came down to it, He was dull and silent to me as I crawled out of bed each morning and started my day. He was moderately big, but what I had of Him in my heart still left me lacking.

I didn't like it. It was lonely, confusing, and exhausting. But somewhere in the middle of all my mess, I caught a glimmer of something. I realized I was being pursued. And I turned to face it. That was a start.

But it took a greater commitment than that to reach out and put my life in the hands of the One who was reaching for me. My heart had to train every ounce of everything I was to look in His direction. It's an expensive eyepiece, the one pointed in God's direction, and to take hold of it was going to cost me everything that I had.

But I chose to see, and like stars punching through the early-evening sky one after the other, slowly the Light began to seep in. It was Light that had been waiting for me for quite a while.

I sat there on the back deck of the cabin, staring at the light glinting off the lake, giving my brain a minute or two to catch up to where the lecture had landed us.

"So, wait. Amy, tell me that part again. How is it possible that a telescope can see farther all the time?"

Once again the science of it all had lost me. It's a wonder I made it through middle school.

"The light the telescope can see has been traveling for years and years to get there."

Whoa. "So you're telling me that the light it's seeing for the first time right this second is light that's been already traveling toward it for years? Maybe even decades?"

"Yep."

Unbelievable. Even before that telescope could see—even before it existed—light was already traveling toward it. It may be that the Hubble is chasing the edge of the universe, but the reality is that the light from the edge of the universe was chasing the telescope way before scientists had even made the plans to put it into orbit. The Hubble has to "choose" to see, yes. But the glory to be seen was always there, always sprinting right down to its level.

And so it goes with us. Before the foundation of the world, before we'd ever breathed, ever dreamed, ever sinned, Light was headed our way. The bigger-than-life Light of the world gave Himself up for us so that we could know the Creator of the edgeless universe and know that He cares what we do with our lives.

He weeps when we hurt. He cares whether or not we have enough to eat or drink today. He sees our deepest dreams, our deepest fears, and He has infinite help to offer us.

WE, MY FRIENDS, ARE INTIMATELY, EXPENSIVELY, AND INTENSELY LOVED.

God's love is a boundless love that barrels in boots toward us every single day. And how we view Him—how His Word makes Him large in our hearts, how His Spirit fills us up with His peace, how His Son steadies us with the assurance that He's overcome the world—changes the way we view our lives. It changes how we deal with grief. It changes how we view our desire for a spouse. It changes the way we see a flat tire, or a lonely holiday, or our checkbook, or an empty womb, or cancer. It changes how we use the good we've been given—our time, our health, our resources.

His universe-size love puts light in our eyes and our hearts. It changes everything. It changes us for the *good*. And all it takes is for us to turn and see.

DESCRIBE SOMEONE YOU KNOW WHO RADIATES A DEEP PEACE IN GOD. IF YOU HAVE EXPERIENCED THIS SAME PEACE, HOW WOULD YOU ADVISE SOMEONE ELSE TO ACCESS IT?

_____

_____

_____

_____

_____

_____

_____

_____

_____

_____

_____

_____

_____

_____

_____

_____

_____

_____

_____

four

WHEN LIFE STARTED TO CHANGE

The Paris Métro rushed along the track, carrying a crowd of silent strangers swaying in unison. As my friend Dana and I and the rest of the passengers bounced around the curves, I gripped my purse and cut my eyes both ways, trying as best as I could without turning all the way around to make sure nobody was hanging around too close to my backpack.

I was probably a little paranoid. But the last time I'd been on the Métro, I'd watched it all go downhill after a well-dressed pregnant girl eased up right next to my dad on the train and held on to the same small handrail he was leaning on.

Shady. Shady McShaderson. *The train is basically empty,* I remember thinking. *There's no need for her to be up in his grill.*

I looked away for a split second and looked back, and

she had her hand in the pocket of his pants fishing for his wallet. I yelled. Dad took in the scene. One second he'd been talking to Mom and enjoying the Eiffel Tower out the window, and the next he turned to find his daughter holding a pregnant girl's hand in his pocket, the two of us locked in a battle of wills.

I won. Being caught in the act was enough to make her withdraw her hand from my grip, say, "Okay, okay," and slink away quickly, and I was thankful for that. Because I'm not sure I could've taken her down. Probably not, let's be real. Despite the fact that she was nearly full term, she looked scrappy. But I would've tried, and I think she saw that in my eyes. You don't mess with my dad.

Months before that when we were getting off the same train, a kid tried to snatch a bag of Skittles from my friend Matt just after he bought it from the vending machine by the subway tracks. The way he yelled, you'd have thought that candy was a money-stuffed wallet. "Nobody takes my Skittles!"

One thing's for sure: that kid sure didn't. And I made a note to myself not to mess with Matt. So because of the Skittles thief—and because of the pregnant girl—I was on full alert the day I stood with all the other people swaying along with the train. I didn't care if my paranoia was obvious. In this sea of businessmen, musicians, tourists, and the elderly, I was ready for anything.

Nobody takes my Skittles. Not if I have anything to say about it.

⟫——————→

But find me on a different day on a train a couple hundred miles north, and I'm a totally different girl.

Just outside London, my bags and my scarf lay strewn across the train's tabletop, my guard down. Paris Paranoia Grace was long gone.

Here, long white passenger trains, ambling through the brilliant green English countryside, threaded quietly through the other locomotives in chunky patterns like thick yarn in winter scarves.

I leaned my head back on the green upholstered seat and watched the scenery sailing past the window. Vivid leaves outside the glass showed the day giving over to the season, the trees reacting to the chilly breeze from the calendar's flip to October. The landscape stretched out, letting in more green, pushing back from the crush of London's buildings, sprawling more and more between small, scattered houses. Quiet filled the train's insides—and seeped into mine too.

Ever since I'd first moved to England, I'd felt like trains were peaceful glass capsules cutting through life, giving me the opportunity to hide myself inside and see the world from a different perspective. Drifting through town after town, I had a clear view of everything from sunshine to storms, from mothers shopping with children to late-night drunken brawls on the train platform. Whether good or bad, I always knew the things I passed through ultimately wouldn't touch me. I was headed somewhere else. And nothing could disrupt the calm inside.

It's funny how your view really can change things, or things can change you, just depending on where and how you stand. Like the Skittles. The Skittles incident changed me. And having my dreams snatched like Skittles changed me too. Before that, I'd just been wide-eyed and naïve, like the world was all sunshine, like I thought nothing would disrupt my norm.

BUT AFTER MY LIFE PLAN WAS RIPPED AWAY, I FELT LIKE EVERYTHING I HAD WAS EXPOSED AND UP FOR GRABS.

The vulnerability turned me into a different person, a person with questions like . . . *What else, God? What else will You take? How do I fix it? And what do I have to do to keep that hurt from happening again?*

I planted my feet and watched my back like that day on the Métro, waiting for someone to take what was mine, which was exhausting. But after a while, something else happened, something that changed my jittery Paris-style self-protection into something more like a ride on a British train.

I found a deep-set quiet nothing could penetrate. And that happened when I felt the light from the God of the universe closing in on me, the glow from Sarah's life beckoning me to dig deeper, to imagine that there was more to be had.

I started asking a different set of questions. *How do I know You like Moses did? Like Sarah did? How do I know You so well that it changes the way I view everything else? How do I get to the point where You really are all I need?*

It was a small start, but it set in motion a radical change.

I remember the moment in my twenties when it happened, when that change began to creep down the tracks and pick up steam. Dawn hadn't begun to crack the sky yet that morning in Alabama, and I sat on my couch with a full cup of tea, enveloped in quiet so thick I felt I could almost hear the steam rising from the cup.

"Okay, God," I whispered. "I'm here. I don't know where to start, but I'm here. And I'm not leaving until we figure this out. I know if You are who You say You are, if everything I've always known and heard about You is true, then my life won't make sense until it's all about You."

In the years since everything I'd built fell apart, I had been trying to get things figured out, get the puzzle pieces back where they were supposed to be. I wished for *something*, the spark that would be the catalyst for change, the lightning bolt that would suddenly bring God from where He stood aloof to a place where I could feel Him. I wanted a shot in the arm that would fill me up with peace and make everything right.

Or at the very least, I wanted the key piece of information that would make everything make sense, that would explain why my life had turned out the way it had. But the spark, the lightning bolt, the shot, the key piece of information—they never came.

So I decided to try a different tactic. That's what brought me to the morning on the couch with a mug of tea and an open Bible in my lap. In a lot of ways, that morning wasn't any different from any other morning. I didn't feel God in a major way. I didn't feel different. But in my heart, something had turned.

I'D REACHED THE POINT OF DESPERATION—DESPERATION NOT SO MUCH FOR ANSWERS BUT FOR GOD HIMSELF.

I wanted God and everything He was, everything He had to offer, at any cost—even though I didn't yet know what that meant. The lifelong faith I'd had in the big God who spoke the world into existence propelled me to try, to do whatever it took. Years of sermons and Bible reading and youth camps and family devotions had piled in decaying stacks in the corners of my soul, the accumulated weight of their teachings looming large. They pressed in desperation against the walls of my heart, begging to either be taken seriously or cleared out.

EITHER HE WAS LIFE-CHANGING OR HE WASN'T. AND DEEP IN MY HEART, I KNEW HE WAS.

This no man's land wasn't good enough anymore. I was exhausted. So I swept the dust from my faith and made my choice. I knew He was pursuing me. I could feel it in the restlessness in my heart, the desire I had for more, the way my mind churned when I lay in bed at night awake. But even though I sensed His pursuit of me, I still didn't know what to do about it.

"God," I whispered, "I'm going to sit here every morning. I'm going to read Your Word for an hour at least. I'm going to pray, not for answers, not for You to send something into my life to make it make sense or to give it direction, but just to know You, to know You for You. To hear You speak. I just want You. I don't want the life I have. If everything I've been taught is true, nothing in my life and nothing that I want is better than me really knowing You. Please show me how to know You. Please show Yourself to me. Please open Your Word to me so that my heart can know You."

It didn't happen in a flash that day, or the next. But I was sincere. And over time, reading God's Word, meditating on it, studying its meaning, and praying desperately for Him to help me know Him better radically changed me. He met me there in His Word and in my deep need. He spoke. His Spirit filled my heart with His Word. My hands held up the broken fragments of dreams, not for Him to repair them or explain them but to replace them with Himself.

I no longer needed an answer from Him for peace. He *was* peace. He became real like nothing had ever been real before; everything else faded away in His light. His Word swept through the corners of my heart, rattled the truths buried there, and aired it out.

And as that happened, tired old clichés snapped to vibrant life. *Trust God. He loves you. Seek God first, and everything else will fall into its proper place. God is good. He is everything you need. Jesus is enough.*

Where along the way did words so electrically profound, so life-changing, become phrases we put on bumper stickers or mumble to each other when we don't know what else to say? Even worse, when did they become words we don't even think about, words we sing in hymns and throw on the dusty pile in our hearts rather than in the furnace of our desire for God? When did they become wallpaper for our faith rather than kindling for the flame?

Once those words—His Word—really took root in my soul, they changed everything. Literally everything. He came to life in my heart, in my day. I began to see my life in light of His love, my steps in light of a destination.

MY HEART CRAVED HIS TRUTH, HIS PRESENCE, AND HE GAVE IT.

My whole life, from the mundane to the chaotic, began to tick around a center rather than career out of control emotionally with me death-gripping the wheel. I'd heard my entire life to "keep Jesus at the center of your life," and I think I believed at times that I was doing that just because of the general sense of awe I had for Him and how that did affect my choices. But until I felt my world picked up and set on the axis of the cross, I didn't really know what that meant.

The big became big, and the small became small. I began to know Him and see His bigness in light of His faithfulness, in light of His love and the story of redemption He so beautifully crafted since the beginning of time.

I began to see Him as a God who knows my every hurt, my every thought, and promises one day to welcome me into a city He's been preparing for me, where I'll never again shed a tear, never again need light shed into the dark corners of my heart. He will be my light and my comfort in a much more complete way than I could ever know here. He will dwell with us. Know us. And we will know Him.

I wished I'd known these truths a lot sooner. I could've saved myself a lot of emptiness.

The empty train lazily crept from the stop, and as it picked up speed, I stretched out in the vacant cabin. Sometimes as the English countryside drifted by the window, I would close my eyes and think about where I'd been. I'd think about the little brick house where God met with me over a cup of tea every morning, a journey that had started that morning I made that first cup and told God I wanted Him at any cost.

I thought about that bed where I lay watching my dreams evaporate from my hands, which felt like a lifetime ago, the distance between a cup full and a cup empty.

In recent months, I'd been thinking a lot about that girl—the girl who lay mourning the loss of what was supposed to be. The one with her heels backed up to that yawning, empty chasm. I thought of all the words I wished I could go back and say to her. I'd tell her that Jesus isn't wallpaper for life but life itself. That you go to God to get God, not to get what God can give.

I'D TELL HER THAT THE ROAD TO A FULL CUP IS LONG AND INVOLVES A LOT OF HARD WORK, BUT THE REWARDS ARE SWEET.

I'd tell her that her life would change on a much deeper level than she could ever imagine. Most of all, I'd tell her that the journey would be worth it. So very, very worth it. And *possible*. Not because of who I am but because of a great, great love. A love for you. A love for me.

Some days I feel like my heart might explode with that reality. *The God of the universe knows us and loves us.* The thought of that truth catches in my chest sometimes when I'm reading in the morning or commuting to work, when I'm cooking dinner or going for a run, when I'm agonizing over loss or when I've received good news. And when it does, it overwhelms me. It's like I can't sing loudly enough, stick my hands in the air high enough, say it well enough to explain how His love wrecks my heart for the better. So much better.

It makes me slam my palms into the ceiling of the car. It makes me nearly crush that teeny tiny communion cup in my hand. I want to shake myself—upset over things that don't matter, wasting hours on pointless stuff—and say *stop*.

I want to go back and tell that girl who was chasing her dreams that there's something better. *Please, stop. Just stop.*

Stop what you're doing and love Him back. He loves you in a way too personal to comprehend. He's for you. He's worth it. And He waits.

In the early morning when the breeze rattles through the window screens and wrinkles the kettle steam, He waits. And I meet Him there. His love, His Word steadies my heart, melts hours away like a conversation over tea with a best friend. He presses His Word on my heart and fills me to the brim with His song. My eyes drink in the breeze-filled morning, and I see Him in the birds He cares for, the flowers He clothes. And He sees me. *The God of the universe sees me and meets me for breakfast.*

He loves us. It's too big. I can't wrap my brain around it. It's bottomless and for the drinking. He winks at us, the thirsty, and bids us come to the well, where we can never know Him too deeply, never ask Him too many times to know Him more. He offers a love paid for with His Son's own humiliation, His own gut-crushing pain, His own loneliness. His own brutal death on a cross. A death He died to pay the price for our sins. *My* sins.

God—the same God who created everything that telescopes will ever see, that light will ever reach—saw fit to become like me in order to win my heart. To win our hearts. He squeezed light-years' worth of glory into a human body and became a man. *For us.*

He took the painful cup of the wrath we deserved for

our rebellion against the Father and drank it to the dregs, knowing that there was life for us at the bottom. He died. And He lives. *So that we can really live.*

He loves us right where we sit, in our own hurt and shame and brokenness and disappointment.

HE STRETCHES OUT A KIND HAND TO REMAKE US.

He bids us to follow Him, leaving everything behind, eyes on Him and on the place He's taking us, a city with a life-giving river that we're urged to drink from for eternity without payment. A place where we need no light of lamp or sun because He Himself is our Light. In His presence, there's fullness of joy. Forever. Comfort for today. Total obliteration of suffering coming just over the horizon.

He loves us. He asks us to put down the things we're clinging to, things that will never fulfill us, and come along. He offers us Himself. He offers us *everything*. And so we make a cup of tea and we meet Him there. We see His love for us. And we plunge.

Plunging isn't what I felt like I was doing that first day I sat down and asked God to show me what it would take to live in His love. It felt more like squeezing my eyes shut, holding my breath, shoving my face into the water and hoping for the best.

I didn't realize that the discipline of meeting with God for the sheer purpose of knowing who God is—not what I should do with my life—would transform my very heart, melt my blindness, and make me see God everywhere I looked. I didn't realize that when His Word showed me who He was, I would feel Him deeply, hear His voice, and trust Him with the kind of trust you reserve for those closest to you.

I didn't realize that when I saw Him in the pages of my Bible and heard His voice speak into my heart, my soul would burst with the realization that there was only one thing I could do with my life. Follow Him. Because of Him. Because of His love. No matter what may come.

I never dreamed it could be like this, that the view of Him passing by, even as a sliver of light on the horizon, a taste of what's still to come, would make me throw my hands open and give all of myself away. With joy.

I NEVER KNEW THAT, WITHOUT DRAGGING MYSELF UP THE STEEP CLIFF OF MENTAL ASSENT AND FORCING IT TO BE SO, GOD REALLY COULD BECOME BIGGER IN MY HEART THAN EVERYTHING ELSE I'D EVER WANTED.

But that's exactly what happened. In my soul, in my life, God was getting bigger all the time. I realized that meant something pretty wonderful for the days still to come. *It meant that it was only going to get better.*

I jumped when my phone buzzed in my pocket that day on the Paris Métro, the day I was standing there in a boxed-out defensive position, ready to take on the masses of wallet and Skittles thieves. I'd texted a couple of my close college friends that day and asked them the question I'd had rolling around in my head and heart.

If you had the chance to go back, what would you tell yourself, the college girl from ten years ago who thought she knew what life was about?

I wondered how they'd respond. Back when we were in college, we'd all seemed to have it together. At the time, I thought I knew what it meant to be solid. I had a lot of stored-up knowledge about God. And I thought I knew the path life was headed down. I wondered if adulthood had rocked my friends the way it had shaken me.

The phone buzzed a couple more times in my pocket, and I pulled it out to see a message thread in progress. My friend Amy B was writing a novel to her college self. And when I read it, I wished I could send it to my college self too. Because it rang true.

Here's what she wrote:

"If I could go back, I would say, 'Amy, that pathway to holiness, that journey to truly deep faith is a lot narrower than you think. And it starts, continues, and ends with a definitive love for the Word of God. I want you to know that what you love now is not really the Word. What you love is what other people tell you about the Word. You love emotion and worship songs and books about God and the social aspect of church in college. But you do not love His Word. Not yet. That takes discipline and study and sacrifice. But you'll get it. You'll begin to put in the hard work of truly studying the Word of God, and when it begins to pay off, your faith will grow into something much more foundational and deep and unexplainable *because you will get real glimpses of who God is on your own*. It will give real strength to your every day because, like A. W. Tozer said, it's when we see Him that we really see ourselves.'"

Amy's words drifted through my head: Deep. Unexplainable. Because you will get real glimpses of who God is on your own. *Because you will straight-up see Him.*

When I loved all the same things Amy said she loved— the social aspect of church, books about God, emotion, and worship songs—I knew the Bible was life-or-death important. I knew it offered hope. Truth. Promises. I think I just believed I was supposed to sift it for any wisdom God might have for the day and then pile anything extra in those dusty corners of my soul for later—background info just in case it was ever needed, or guidelines for what to do and what not to do.

I DON'T THINK I REALLY EXPECTED TO SEE HIM, OR FOR MY HEART TO EXPAND AS I KNEW HIM MORE. I SAW THE BIBLE AS STATIC, HIS LOVE IN MY LIFE AS STATIC.

Both are constant and unchanging. That part's true. But they aren't stationary. His Word is a slicing two-edged sword, and His love drives people to the death. Willingly. I think I knew that, and somehow I still never expected them to wreck me like they did, to totally remake me, to change my whole life. But they did. They still are.

God's love is a foreign language to that girl still trapped in her broken dreams back in that bed in Alabama, the one with the really bland dictionary of God's love and what that love feels like, but if I could go back, I'd tell her to hang in there.

As Amy said, *You don't see it yet, but you'll get it*. It's there for the seeing, for the discovering. For the grasping. Press on, and press on at any cost. *It only gets better from here.*

HAVE YOU EVER ASKED GOD THIS QUESTION: HOW CAN I
KNOW YOU SO WELL THAT IT CHANGES THE WAY I VIEW
EVERYTHING ELSE? WHAT ACTIONS IN YOUR LIFE SHOWED
THAT YOU SERIOUSLY WANTED AN ANSWER MORE THAN
ANYTHING ELSE?_____

_____

_____

_____

_____

_____

_____

_____

_____

_____

_____

_____

_____

_____

_____

_____

five

BETTER THAN OUR DREAMS

"Eat your eggs, and watch your back."

Those were the instructions that came with my thirtieth birthday breakfast in the mountains of Maryland. Breakfast gets weird fast when you order Granny's scrambled eggs and then eat them while people browse her extensive firearm inventory displayed on the walls all around you. They're tasty eggs, but you eat them without looking down while both eyes scan the room.

I guess that's what happens when you don't have a plan—you end up eating the most important meal of the day at a café and gun shop in one. The day before our breakfast at gunpoint, my friend Emily and I had left before dawn and driven several hours to middle-of-nowhere Maryland, apparently the only place in the Northeast with a real live dude ranch. I'll admit that I was surprised there was one up there at all. I'd always thought of Maryland as more crab cake than cowboy. But there was one. And for a low, low price, you could be a cowgirl for a day, taught the ropes—literally—by Maryland's most elderly cowboy.

Calf roping. Cattle herding. Cutting. Sold.

That's how I ended up spending my birthday having lunch at a tiny Irish pub in the Maryland countryside with Emily and Grandpa Gunslinger. And that's how we ended up having our eggs the next day in Granny's gun cabinet. We just wanted to get away for a little while. Do something different. And over coffee that morning, we both agreed we'd succeeded. Past that, we had no further plans—just a whole lot of time.

It was cool in a way. We didn't feel locked into anything. Plans are good, but they can tie you down sometimes. This way, Maryland was a blank slate, with just us and Google to determine our next move. That style of living can be scary to the planner types, but it also has the potential to be awesome.

IT'S THAT WAY WITH MOST BLANK SLATES: THEY HAVE THE POTENTIAL TO BE BOTH EXCITING AND UNPREDICTABLE.

I felt that way about adulthood too. It sounded a little scary, but it had the potential to be awesome.

But there's a big difference between the way Em and I were traveling through Maryland and the way this blank-slate life was meant to be navigated. Adulthood may be a clean canvas with a crazy huge paint selection, but it isn't just a fly-by-the-seat-of-your-pants trip or a journey to wherever you might end up.

It needs something driving it. And that something isn't a map, or a new plan, or a revived dream. It's a destination.

Emily and I topped the hill in the late-afternoon sunlight near the Appalachian Trail, and there it was—the screened-in tree house we had decided would be our landing place for the night. We just didn't know a lot of other transplants in the area had the same idea. Not until we saw the bright-yellow note taped to the door.

Hey, Grace and Emily. It seems that because of the unseasonable heat wave, we have a stinkbug infestation this week in the area. We vacuumed out your tree house around 3:00 p.m., and we'll be back before sunset to see if we missed any.

Missed any. The inside of the tree house was nothing but stink bugs. In the couple of hours since the three o'clock Shop-Vac visit, a solid curtain of reinforcements had already amassed on the inside of the screen door where the note was hung.

I looked at Emily. Without hesitation she shook her head. "Mm-mm. No way."

I was with her on this one. Things had just become

a little too crazy. We both knew we were going to do this thing spontaneously and see where we ended up. But neither of us knew we were driving straight into a stinkbug apocalypse. That night we negotiated a fancy furnished cabin from the campground manager, who seemed to feel genuinely sorry for us. But in Emily's recounting of the story, even the cabin was crawling with the East's least-welcome party crashers.

If it was, I didn't care. I was beyond exhausted. I crawled into bed—a bed she says actually had stinkbugs in it—and passed out cold. The next morning I found out that she'd spent half the night up, shaking them out of the sheets and the curtains. The other half of the night she'd spent in bed with tissue stuffed in her ears and a sock tied over her mouth.

The comment never came from her mouth, but I'm guessing the next day she thought it: *blessed are those who make reservations at normal hotels.*

Nobody can say I don't plan a great party.

And that was only the beginning.

The tent peg shook in my hand as I tried to push it deeper into the ground. Nothing. The ground was super hard. That peg wasn't going anywhere.

"I don't think it will matter if we can't pin it down well," Emily said from over by the fire. "There's a zero percent chance of precipitation tonight. Zero! That never happens. This is going to be awesome! We can even leave the rainfly off the top of the tent."

After the stinkbug incident, we had pooled our money and sprung for a night in a nice hotel near Baltimore Inner Harbor. But tonight we found ourselves back out on the land. Hot. But no bugs. We could work with that.

As the fire crackled just enough for a little light and a lot of s'mores, we talked about life, drilling down from light to deep. Astronomy. Bears. Aging. Dreams. God.

Many times in the past, Emily had brought me back to truth when my emotions were all over the place. Many times she'd reminded me of the bigger picture, the greater overarching story taking place around the plot twist I was panicking over.

Many times she'd been willing to take a topic and drive it deep, playing devil's advocate, asking the tough questions just so we could argue it out and have a more balanced understanding about why we thought what we thought, pinning down a little better why we believed what we believed. Like what was at the center of the God/dreams equation. And what's really happening when you pray faithfully for something—something good, like a husband—and it never comes along. Those kinds of things can eat at your soul if you don't get them out in the open. With friends. With God.

"When you look at it logically, we were designed to be married and have families. God built us that way," Emily said during one of these conversations. "I don't know why God would create us that way, give us those dreams all our lives, and then not fulfill them after we've prayed for them for years."

She'd picked a tricky topic to unpack. This was a touchy one for me too. I'd prayed those prayers. We both had. Emily knew that. This definitely wasn't our first rodeo on this subject. And we both needed our hearts firmed up.

"I think what we have to go back to and rest in is the fact that His heart for us is good," I said. "We know that everything we do here is aimed at preparing us for the day we step into His kingdom.

"So that means that anything we go through here— loneliness or persecution or whatever—is an opportunity to trust one more time in His deep love for us.

"Marriage is meant to help point us to God in this life, but He's going to give us what we need to sustain us through this part no matter what. That may mean a husband, but it may not.

"But we're told that if we persevere through all the things that happen in our lives here and trust Him through it, then at the end of it, we get Him. And that's what we aim for."

"I get that," Emily said. "But I already *have* Him."

True.

Silence reigned for a minute or two. It *was* true. I'd felt the sentiment myself. But something about its flatness didn't settle right in my heart. Hers either. Of course, we *do* already have Him. That's a promise. We have the promise of His love, His faithfulness, His Spirit living and working in us if we accept the gift of life He extends to us and choose to follow Him.

He has us, and we have Him. That will never change. But at the same time, if we already have God now in the exact same way we will have Him one day, why would striving for Him or longing for Him do us any good? If we already have all of Him that there is to be had and we still feel the aching empty spaces in our lives, the gaping cracks in the temporary earthly tents we live in, what can fill them?

That sort of thinking would set us up to believe that obviously He can't fill those cracks by Himself, so He's going to have to use something else. Like a spouse. A family. A job that gives us purpose. In this equation, that can be the only logical answer. Right? My heart turned uneasily in my chest. *It can't be.*

If that were true, it would mean that it was possible to exhaust who God is and that the world still has more to offer us. It would mean that something we could have or do or be would make us more alive than He can make us. It would turn things that God designed to point us to Him into things we expect Him to give us in order to fill the holes we hold Him responsible for creating. It would make those things ends in themselves.

Can He use those earthly parts of our lives to teach us, prepare us? Yes. Can He show us more of Himself, more of His love through them? Definitely. Didn't He *design* marriage to be a picture of the gospel, the love between Christ and His Church? Yes, and it's beautiful. Didn't He design raising kids and working purposeful jobs to mold our hearts to be more like Him and to share Him with others? Yes.

But does His design make those things *necessary* for us to see His goodness fill us up to the brim with love, peace, joy? Are we doomed to a half-life if we don't have them? I don't think He ever said that or meant for it to be that way. That would make Him a pretty small God.

I was glad Emily said what she said, about how we already have Him, so why was the idea of getting Him later all that life-changing? Her words struck a nerve in my heart because I'd had the same feelings before but never consciously realized it. I'd lived my life like He was a small God, which changes everything.

A LOT HINGES ON WHETHER WE SEE GOD AS A MEANS TO AN END OR AN END IN HIMSELF.

There's a big difference between our hearts sprinting the short distance home to see our beloved God face-to-face and our hearts meandering through the stretching expanse of life with God in our pocket, not really thinking much about where we'll end up. That's exactly how I'd treated Him in the past, like a pocketful of Him was what I had now and all I'd ever have. So my dissatisfaction roamed around here on earth looking for fulfillment, looking for something God made but not God Himself.

No. I've lived like it before, but I refuse to believe it. I refuse to believe my God is that small. There has to be something greater than just having God tucked safely in our pockets, cruising along through life until the day we can take Him out and see Him face-to-face.

There's got to be more of a driving plot to this thing than the way Em and I planned Maryland, not knowing where we'd be sleeping at the end of the day. There's got to be more to our lives than just filling our time, satiating our palate with the next good thing and looking to God like He's TripAdvisor, offering suggestions here and there. This story has got to be building toward a really, really grand apex.

We lay there in the tent staring through the sheer roof, the stars stretching far and wide and brilliant. Brighter than the campfire. More numerous than the stinkbugs. *How can we not be consumed with the feeling that our lives are made for something so much bigger?* I thought. The flimsy tent we were in was the perfect picture—all it would take was one good storm to finish it off. It was weak and uncomfortable. It couldn't be more temporary. As long as we're in these "tents" we groan, being burdened with them and their limitations and weaknesses and lack. Scripture tells us that in 2 Corinthians 5.

So we have to go to something to be filled. God couldn't have intended for that to be something earthly. If He had, surely Jesus wouldn't have been so deliberate to emphasize the importance of food you can't see, the fact that bread alone can't fill our appetites, the reality that living water is the only thing that will satiate our thirst.

He wanted us to keep returning to Him over and over and over to be filled until the day that a drink from the river of the water of life in heaven fills us up, never to be thirsty again. He wanted us to store our treasures there. Not here. That means valuing Christ above everything. And that means keeping what we long for with natural longings—like marriage and kids—in their proper places.

In light of eternity, the longest marriage seems short. Grief lasts but for a night. Our whole lives—all the hard times and good moments—will be over in a breath. The greatest sacrifice seems small. And God seems really, really big.

NO MATTER WHAT WE DO HERE, NO MATTER HOW WE LIVE LIFE—MARRIED OR SINGLE, CHILDLESS OR RAISING A HERD OF KIDS, DOING AN ACCOUNTING JOB OR DIGGING WELLS IN AFRICA—WE DO IT TO KNOW GOD AND TO GET HIM.

Take marriage, for one. Francis Chan wrote a whole book about how marriage should be valued, but valued in light of how it prepares us for eternity. God should be the prize of marriage rather than marriage the prize we get from God.

It's not just semantics. It's a change that can seep into your heart, center your life, and change the way you view the desires you have that go unfulfilled while you're living in this earthly tent. The felt needs begin to make you long for more of Him. They make you ask to know Him better rather than asking Him to send things other than Himself to fill them in.

Our affection becomes fixed on Him in a way that causes our needs to take their proper places in our hearts. Do we still feel them sometimes? Sure. We're human. And don't get me wrong—we can and should pray for our physical needs. Jesus Himself taught us to pray for our daily bread. He cares about our needs, knows us intimately, and is the Giver of all good gifts in our lives. He's the God who would never give His son or daughter a stone when he or she asks for bread.

But when it comes down to it, the thing Jesus led with in His prayer just after pure worship was "Your kingdom come." That's the higher objective—to have Him and His kingdom as our destination, our goal. To sprint with every breath toward the moment we see God's face. To ask Him how to know Him better here in order to make the best use of the time, to breathe most deeply of His grace. And to ask Him to come sooner. Please, please come sooner. *Man cannot live on bread alone.*

For a long time, life for me hadn't really felt like a story building steam toward a destination, a life spent yearning for the day I got to look my Savior in the face. It hadn't felt like every step was building toward that, with me watching where He walked and following closely, knowing His love as my own and trusting that the best was yet to come.

Instead, life felt more like a journey with no set place to finish, a long, long stretch of years spent meandering around the map, like I was carrying Him with me to the finish line. There in my pocket, His brightness dimmed, His footsteps ahead of mine disappeared. And in the space where He should've been, earthly desires shifted into my line of sight. It was a lot more like He was just there close at hand to talk to occasionally and to ask the "why" questions. It was a lot less like He was actively leading me to the real life He'd had for me all along—life in Himself. Life where He dwells with us and calls us beloved daughters and sons *face-to-face.* If we don't realize how big the kingdom on the horizon is, we run the risk of feeling that God is really small here. And if the light on the horizon isn't so bright it's nearly tangible, the small here can become really, really big.

There's got to be a grand delineation between the kingdom of God that is on earth and the kingdom that's still to come. And it's got to be strong enough to pull our hearts up from our broken dreams here with an insatiable draw toward what will be. There's got to be hope. We've got to know He desires good for us. Here on earth, sure. He fills us up to the brim with His peace, His joy, His love. He hurts when we hurt. And He *knows* how we hurt. He's been there too. But there's got to be real hope that transcends our broken world and longs—really *longs*—for the real life He is preparing for us in the world to come. He has to be worth it. Worth fixing our eyes on. Worth trading everything here for.

The whole thing is ultimately rigged for our good, with the best possible ending. It makes our hearts soar *here*. It changes the way we view everything. It washes even the most broken path golden like a Colorado sunrise.

AS WE WALK THE ROAD DELIBERATELY WITH HIM, TOWARD HIM, WE WATCH HIM WRITE OUR STORY WITH LOVE AND PURPOSE, TO KNOW HIM A LITTLE BETTER, TO FEEL THE LIGHT A LITTLE BRIGHTER.

The good that God has for our lives in Himself isn't a consolation prize, something we comfort ourselves with if we don't have the earthly things we want most. It's the destination our hearts have been longing for since the day we were created. The road there may turn out to look way, way different than we imagined. But He assures us . . . it will be *better*.

I felt it on my face. A tiny perforated splash. Rain. On that "zero percent chance of precipitation" night, we went from zero to awake in seconds.

Where is the rainfly? I had no idea. We stumbled around outside the tent in our pajamas until we found it, secured it over the tent, and fell back inside wet and laughing.

It was unexpected, to say the least. But the fact that it was unplanned only made it better.

A BLANK SLATE BECOMES A WHOLE DIFFERENT DEAL WHEN WE REALIZE THE PEN THAT'S WRITING THIS WILD AND BEAUTIFUL STORY IS IN THE HAND OF A GOD WHO LOVES US AND IS CREATING A PLOT WITH HUGE PAYOFF AT THE END.

And that payoff is *Him*. Each drop of unplanned rain, each plate of eggs, each day spent as a rookie cowgirl is part of a grand narrative, a tale that puts purpose in our earthly "tents" but even greater purpose beyond them. And that purpose is way better than any dreams we could've come up with on our own.

As we lay there in that rain-splattered tent in Maryland, Emily said what I was thinking: "I'm pretty sure this has gone down as one of the best trips of my life, though it wasn't at all what I thought it would be."

"Me too, Em. Me too."

DESCRIBE HOW, IN YOUR LIFE, YOU HAVE EITHER VIEWED GOD AS SOMEONE YOU'RE STRIVING FOR, OR SOMEONE YOU HAVE IN YOUR POCKET TO RIDE WITH YOU THROUGH LIFE._____

_____

_____

_____

_____

_____

_____

six

PUTTING OUR DREAMS WHERE THEY BELONG

The few leaves still lingering on the trees rustled as the breeze passed through the screened-in porch and into the house. The air was laden with gorgeous golden silence out here in the Birmingham suburbs, the kind of peace that—after six months of living in the middle of a swarming city—feels like a big, warm hug. I sipped my tea. I listened. Nothing. *Man, it's beautiful.*

The only sound I heard at all was a little clatter every time the wind blew through the front porch just right and caught the big orange wooden *T* that hung on the front door.

Monograms are a big deal here in the South. They're everywhere. My sister embroiders them like crazy, and she's not the only one. It's the gift everybody gives at bridal and baby showers. Monogrammed towels. Monogrammed onesies. Monogrammed hats and shirts and bags. It's a little out of control. But I like them. And I like that big orange *T*—for my friend Elizabeth's surname—hanging on the front door of her house.

The other day when she and I were in the middle of a serious discussion, we left to go get some food. When she locked the door behind us, the *T* rattled against it as we walked away.

"This is probably really dumb sounding," she said, "but the idea of my name staying the same was a difficult thing for me for a while."

To her, the fact that her name never changed was a visible mark of her single state. Every time a newly married friend went out shopping for new monograms, it was a reminder that life looked the same as it always had. I think all of us probably have markers like that—like friends' wedding pictures on social media, or a mailbox full of family-photo Christmas cards—things that remind us of a dream that didn't quite work out, that the life we've always wanted hasn't yet materialized—and that it might never. For a good number of us, that's not been an easy thing to stomach. We wake up, and the reminders are still there.

I had a reminder like that, one I picked out myself and slipped on my finger when I was sixteen. It was simple, gold with the words *true love waits* etched around the band. That mantra was the thing when we were in youth group, part of a popular movement to encourage teenagers to commit to save sex for marriage. The rings were meant to be a reminder of that pledge to God and to our future spouses. I remember thinking when I put mine on for the first time that it was a little bit sacred, a symbol of sincerity and chastity. Both good things.

But without my realizing it, the whole concept spun deeper issues in my soul. That gold ring wormed its way into my heart in a way I didn't see coming. It became a symbol of hope—hope for the life I wanted one day. It reminded me that I had something to *wait* for—love, marriage, life as a family.

And my heart started tapping its foot . . . and kept tapping well into adulthood.

I did what I was supposed to do. Shouldn't God have brought me someone by now? Is this who He is? Because if this is who He is, I don't know if I want any part of it.

And I don't think I was alone in that.

It's a graveyard of hearts, the place where singles in their mid-twenties and older start waking up to the reality that a lot of the things we've always dreamed of aren't really panning out.

THAT REALIZATION AFFECTS EACH OF US A LITTLE DIFFERENTLY.

But there's a massive common wound that many carry, whether or not they realize it right away, whether or not they say it out loud.

We're not sure who God really is anymore.

God—or who we thought God was—had a lot to say when we were younger about how our lives should go, like how we should "wait" until marriage, until He brought the right person along, which can be challenging for a teenager. It can take a lot for youth leaders to get buy-in for that sort of commitment. But those leaders had something on their side when they made that sell—there was a finish line, a destination. Marriage.

Wait, and the spouse will come. Seek God, and He'll bring you the person He has for you.

Pretty words. They put a spark of hope in the eyes of a high school kid needing something to look forward to, something to help push past the pressure or the loneliness, to know there was something better coming.

Just wait. Live your life for God, and wait.

Find that kid still single ten or fifteen or thirty years later, and in his or her eyes you may see a tiny, flickering flame struggling desperately to hold on to faith—if it hasn't already been snuffed out altogether. Because the destination planted in that kid's heart wasn't God. It was a person, a dream. A dream of a life that never came. A life that would've never offered ultimate fulfillment even if it had.

$$\gg\!\!\longrightarrow$$

Marriage. That's just one dream. There are a hundred others like it. They may not all have a gold ring to go with them, but they're chiseled in our hearts, the golden ideas of the life we want, of what God should have for us in the here and now. Like good health. Good jobs. A family. Purposeful lives.

They're all good desires. But if we aren't careful about how we carry them, they can tank our faith in ways we never saw coming when we slipped that gold "promise" into our hearts and said we would follow God in obedience . . . and wait.

It's not a new problem. It's happened to God's people from the moment we were first set free to dream. Take these guys, for example: when God brought His chosen people, Israel, out of slavery in Egypt, a lot of crazy things happened. There were plagues, water turned to blood, and God parted the Red Sea. Massive historical moments. Miraculous feats. The Israelites got to see God act in a big, big way. But in the midst of all those grandiose things going on in the story, it's easy to miss one of the more subtle crazy things that happened.

As the Israelites finally prepared to run from the place that had been holding them captive, they turned to the people of Egypt who lived around them and asked them for their clothes and jewelry . . . and the people of Egypt just handed them their stuff.

This was a gift from God. He had told them that would happen. So they left Egypt with their pockets jingling with gold, a promise of blessings to come.

The Israelites probably had some ideas as to how that gold could be used. They had big plans to build a new life in the land God had promised them. But He had something greater in mind than their plans. That treasure was earmarked from the beginning with a purpose the people couldn't even see, something greater than they could've ever imagined or wished for. Because eventually *giving it away* was how *they got to see God live among them.*

One day God was going to ask them to give without holding back so that the tabernacle could be built—"a sanctuary; that I may dwell among them" (Exodus 25:8 KJV). This was why He'd purchased their freedom—so He could live with them, and they with Him. To make that happen, they were going to *have the privilege* of giving away their most precious possessions so that they could have a part in bringing God's kingdom and presence into their midst.

Gold and silver were special. God knew that. So did the people—but they didn't quite have the same reasons in mind. Over the miles, they probably liked the way that gold jingled in their pockets. They saw the way the other people in the land around them were living nice lives in the here and now with what they'd built with their gold. And since the Israelites didn't really have a daily, overwhelming sense of what they were building in the future, the present looked worth investing everything in.

They wanted something tangible, something immediate. They couldn't see God right then. So they decided to take some of their gold, use it to make a statue of a calf, and call it their god. When I hear that story, it sounds ridiculous at times. How could they leave a God who parted the Red Sea for them just because they didn't understand what He was doing? How could they put everything they had into a golden calf instead? It seems insane. But we do it too.

It happens when we lose sight of who God is—our dreams make their way from our pockets into our hearts, and God moves from our hearts into our pockets. And the jingle of our dreams becomes a lot louder than His voice.

That's when we find ourselves in real danger. Our dreams become idols, and we start thinking of taking matters into our own hands, of spending our lives the way we think is best in order to achieve our dreams. Either that or we sit there stubbornly, allowing the jingling to drown out His voice until He's barely audible, or not audible at all. And we become bitter.

We have to face this: both will kill us. We all have a dream that's the big deal for us personally, the one that tries to well up in our hearts and be bigger than God.

You know what yours is. I know what mine is. It's the

dream we have etched in gold in our hearts, the thing our gut-level humanity sees and wants and thinks is *really worth the wait*. The struggle is real, and it's time we face it with some real truth. It's time we put some teeth to the advice to *live for God, wait and good things will come*.

Because the reality is that it's *true*, so long as we really understand what the good things are that we are aiming for. Moses, the Israelites' leader, knew what that good was. He had *seen* it. His face glowed with it. Glowed because of God. That God—the One who's bigger than the mountains and the universe, the One who sprints to us with all-consuming love—*He's* the treasure, not the dreams jingling in our pockets. *He's* the good we should live our lives straining for.

And it's a razor-edge nuance that makes all the difference. To live for God. Or to live *for* God. Living for God *includes* God in the life we have and what we want for our lives. It thanks God for the gold and lives to please Him *so that* we can build a good life.

BUT LIVING *FOR* GOD ORDERS OUR HEARTS AND EVERYTHING WE HAVE TOWARD WINNING GOD.

It holds out with open, outstretched hands what we have and what we'd like to see happen. Living *for* God forms our hearts to want to spend our gold on seeing Him come. It sees our dreams as tools in His hand to use as He pleases, for our good and for His glory. And that changes *everything*. Everything about our lives. Everything about our hearts.

Jesus makes a point to tell us that the gate is narrow, the way hard to get God in the end. He says, "Those who find it are few" (Matthew 7:14). I think I always thought He meant that few people would be able to stick with following God's rules. Keeping ourselves holy. *Waiting*. Things like that. That's part of it. Being made holy, made more into Christ's likeness is hugely part of it. And living in obedience is vital.

But the gate to everything good is narrow for a bigger reason. It's about more than what we do. It's about what we *love*. It's about what we want, what we seek, what's at the core of our desire. It's about us living our lives with Him as the dream, with all our hopes aiming for the purpose He's marked our life with. It's about what we *do* flowing out of who we *love*.

It means putting in all our chips to see God *live with us*, whatever He asks. Everything is on the table. It means dying to self. That, my friends, is the hard part.

IN ORDER TO GET HIM, OUR DREAMS AND BEST-LAID PLANS HAVE TO DIE ON THE ALTAR OF OUR LOVE FOR HIM.

And that goes against the way we're brought up to live in this place. Our hearts have been ordered to crave what we see here. And they've been that way since we were young.

I remember when I was that high school student "waiting," when I was living for God, but not to *get* God. I remember what my prayers and desires sounded like. And high-school Grace's prayers are pretty easy to decode. *Please, Jesus, don't come back until I get married. At least let me be married for a little while.*

It makes me laugh a little when I think about it. How could I have ever thought anything here was worth postponing seeing God, seeing His kingdom come? My view of God as a treasure to be won was small. But are my prayers any different in adulthood when I stare Him in the face and tell Him I don't understand His choices for my life, that I think my earthly dreams are worth more of my heart space than He is? They might be more complicated prayers, but the heart issue is still the same. *I'd rather spend my heart's gold on me than on His kingdom.*

There was a guy I'd liked for years who got my gold before I even realized that was possible, before I knew God had something much, much bigger in mind for it.

This guy was deep. Godly. Hilarious. Smart. And a

great friend. The night I realized he liked me, my dreams were jingling long and loud in my pocket. We were sitting on the cusp of the real world, outside on the curb. The southern humidity was rolling in for the summer and hanging in the late-night air around us, but the sky was clear as a bell. And I saw something happen.

I SAW THE STARS ALIGN.

And I saw all the dreams flash before my eyes that I'd been praying about all those mornings in college as I read my Bible and ate Reese's Puffs. I'd been asking God what to do with my life. I'd prayed for a husband. I didn't know how it was going to happen exactly, but I still expected that it wouldn't be all that long before the house and the 2.5 kids and the career I'd always wanted would pan out. I was considering a few jobs for after graduation—one of which was overseas—and I was excited about *all* of them. The world was wide open. I was thrilled.

Now this guy I really liked sat next to me, praying for both of our futures, and I couldn't contain the smile, the happiness that washed over my heart. *This is everything I've ever wanted. Thank You, God.* I tiptoed back into the dorm room past my sleeping roommate, and I went to bed smiling. I don't think I slept at all, and I fell asleep during our graduation the next day. No idea who the speaker was. No idea what happened. But I walked away knowing I had my whole life ahead of me, and gosh, it looked awesome.

The weeks and months that followed were a lovesick blur. Finally, this whole store of feelings I'd had for this guy for so long came rushing out, breaking the dams I'd built in my heart, washing the whole world a rosy color. And in the middle of that, something happened. I tucked God in my pocket, and I said, *Thanks, I can take it from here.*

I didn't mean to. If you had asked me if that was happening, I would've straight denied it. I thought God and I were in a really good place when everything started going so well. But He had never become bigger to me than the tangible desires, so when they all came together perfectly, I let Him sit out a couple of plays. He wasn't the destination; He was the means to it, even though I don't think I could've articulated that. My life with this guy was everything I wanted, and I wanted God to be a part of that life, but I thought it was going to drive itself from here, or that we were going to all drive it together.

My life with God got shallow, really shallow. The life I wanted on earth became a whole lot bigger. And over time, something happened to my heart. I couldn't hear His voice. The jingling of my dreams in my heart was really, really loud. My love was poured entirely on a person first, and the trickle left for God at the end of the day was growing smaller and smaller.

That's where selfishness began to take root in my heart and choke out the God who loved me and wanted *all* my love for Himself, and for any other love I gave out on earth to flow out of my love for Him. I can imagine selfishness looked pretty ugly on me.

Pretty soon, everything began to unravel. I remember where it ended just as vividly as where it began. He and I were standing on a porch in the same late-night southern humidity, not knowing how to untangle the mess that had come from what had started as such a blessing. I found out what happens to my heart when my eyes drop from a holy God to a golden calf I've made for myself. It's not pretty.

And the next thing I knew, I was waking up to that pile of tissues and broken dreams.

The form my idol took was pretty obvious in a relationship. But it was a lot more subtle in singleness. Those same desires—the ones for a marriage, a family, a home—stayed way too big in my heart even after the smoke from the failed relationship had cleared and left nothing but ashes behind.

I sheepishly approached God again. I knew I'd really messed up. But even as I asked forgiveness for my selfishness and prayed and asked for a fresh start, I approached Him the same way I did in college. *God, help me know how to build my life. Help me know what to do, where to go from here. Please help me to live for You. And please bring me what You have for me.*

It wasn't until much later I realized that my unfulfilled dreams can choke out God just as much as the tangible realization of those dreams, if not more so. My heart wanted what He could give way more than it wanted just Him. And I'll admit . . . I didn't realize how wrong that was. I thought that was the way it was supposed to work, that we "love" God and are obedient to Him, and He builds our lives here. I could never figure out why that just didn't feel right, why my heart never felt ordered correctly, why the restlessness in my heart didn't feel like the good kind of restlessness.

GOD HAD TO BE BIGGER THAN THIS, BIGGER THAN THE SUPERVISOR OF MY BLUEPRINTS, BIGGER THAN THE GOD WHO BRINGS THE LIFE I WANT ON A PLATTER AS A REWARD FOR MY OBEDIENCE.

He had to be bigger, or He was never going to rise above the earth's tangible dreams in my heart. I was never going to love Him more, not with the kind of love that washed my world rosy when the guy I liked started to pursue me, not with the kind of love that has way more depth and realness than even that.

I was only going to "love" Him with the churchy kind of "love" that didn't really feel like anything, the kind that acknowledges He's in charge and kind of a big deal. But that was just never going to work. I wanted Him to get my real love, my real gold. So at twenty-five, I took off the ring I'd worn since I was sixteen. I didn't tell anyone I was doing it. I just slipped it off my finger that day and, before tucking it away in a box, ran my finger around the words on the band. *Wait*, I remember thinking. *What's it "waiting" for, anyway?*

I DIDN'T WANT TO WAIT ANYMORE. I ALREADY HAD GOD. AND HE IS EVERYTHING.

For me, taking off that ring needed to happen. To a lot of people, a ring like that carries a good meaning. It really *can* be a solid reminder of a commitment to God and to purity. And that's great. Purity given to God is a holy sacrifice, when it's given to Him *for* Him. And purity is vital to marriage. It's a good commitment to make.

But for me, that ring symbolized that I expected something of God that He had never promised. It underscored the wrong view I had of the Person whom I loved most. The ring was building a golden calf for me, and that's something it should never do. So even though for some people putting the ring *on* is a symbol of letting go of desires, for me, taking it *off* was. Because I was saying to God that I was going to be obedient, and that the only thing I wanted from my obedience was Him, not what He would reward me with here on earth. I was saying He was the One worth spending everything I had on, just because of who He is. I wanted Him to know I trusted Him with my story. And I wanted to give Him permission to write it differently than what I'd outlined for myself.

I told Him that *He* was my desire, which brought freedom. Freedom to live without waiting for something to start. Freedom to love Him and hold things here with a very loose grip. *Freedom to dream new dreams.* Freedom for Him to show me how those dreams were far better than any I'd ever had before. And He did. He showed me that.

Over time, His dreams—the desire for me to know Him better, to love what He loves, and to spend my life chasing Him—became the air my soul breathes. The more I get, the more I want. It's a desire that's both *real* and *right*. And that *feels amazing.* It washes the world with the kind of brilliant color only He can paint. When the freedom came rolling in, the freedom that resulted from Him occupying my whole heart, the sky became clear and everything aligned—*for real.* I saw it happen—a distinct change in the air, in the world, in my heart.

Thank You, God. This is better than everything I've ever wanted.

But this clarity didn't come overnight. The makings of it rode around in my pocket for a while. I talked about it over lunch with people, I thought about it on my commute to work, and I let it marinate for a really long time before urgency finally pushed it to the surface and said, *Now's the time. You can't really live without it.*

After months of hearing my pastor in Birmingham stress how a love for God is cultivated by a love for His Word, I finally went all in. My pastor was right. It took discipline. Persistence. Sincerity. But through the days, weeks, and months, the trickle became a bucketful, and I drank from it like I hadn't had water in years. Or ever. *It's become my life.*

The God who's bigger than the universe finally became big in my heart. And when He did, my heart followed, and so did my obedience. The two go hand in hand. We know, we love, and we follow. The more I know Him, the more I'm able to talk with Him, able to ask more of what I know He wants for me. *You love me, God. You know me, You hear me, and You're working things for my good and Your glory. I know this is true. Please spend my life the way You want to, the way that's best for Your kingdom. My life is Yours. I just want to know You more.*

It's a different kind of prayer than the blueprint prayers of the years of my broken dreams.

Thank You, God. Thank You for what You've done for me. For who You are. For what You're doing in the world with Your story, and how You let me be a part of it.

I say out loud my love for Him, and it reminds my heart of what my life here is about. I ask Him to expand my heart to love Him more and more.

I love You, Father. I love You more than my family or my friends. I want You more than I want a husband or a purposeful job or to live abroad. I want You more than I want my own comfort or a car or a vacation or a nice place to live.

It's a simple—but surprisingly effective—type of prayer that I learned from my friend Scott. "My practice," he wrote once, "is to (out loud or in my head) tell Christ all the things He is more important than. Like 'You are more important than TV or the Internet. You are more important than my parents or brother. You are more important than my wife or my job.' It really helps me focus."

It helps me too. I pour out my heart to God, to this One who is more important than my family or friends or the Internet or my dreams. I read His Word slowly and let it wash over me. I learn who He really is so that when the enemy and the world try to whisper lies, I see them for what they are.

You haven't abandoned me. You'll never leave me. You love me. Nothing is worth more than You.

Every morning I see it. First thing. My friend Candice made it for me—a black canvas with white lettering and a ring of green garland painted around it. I love it, and I put it on the wall in a spot where it's the first thing I see every morning.

The words on the canvas are from the first line of an Audrey Assad song called "Good to Me," a song about how nothing that happens, nothing I have or don't have, can steal my joy when I have God. Every morning it reminds me of where my hope comes from, where my steadiness comes from, no matter what the day brings. The bedrock truth of His promise. The steadfast ground of His goodness. *Hallelujah. Those things will never change.*

Those are the type of reminders I'm hanging in my life and my heart these days—the ones that point me to God as the destination my whole life is sprinting toward. I want Him. I need Him to get through the day.

I NEED HIM TO FILL UP MY HEART WITH HIS STEADY LOVE, HIS TRUTH, HIS DESIRES.

That happens when I know Him and remind myself of who He is.

My heart is changed. My plans take their proper place,

and He becomes my everything. The new dreams He starts to write for me are the ones that lead me straight toward Him. And they start with His Word. It's love and discipline working together that draw me to meet with Him in the morning, to read the Bible, to study, to meditate, to memorize His Word and write it on my heart. I memorize the truths that my heart needs to be reminded of the most. My friend Heather held me accountable to that last year and encouraged me to quote 2 Corinthians 4–5 to her over honey biscuits at our favorite coffee shop once a week until I could say it all.

That challenge drove me deeper into the Word and deeper in love with God. Those chapters reminded me that no matter how much we as "jars of clay" are pressed, we are not crushed—God's strength fills us when we are weak. And God has far better in store in the days to come if we can just hang on.

Thank God that the Holy Spirit taught that to my heart through His Word. When a close friend died a few months later, that truth became air when I could barely breathe. But even in that, I saw God not just keeping me afloat—He took the ashes and made them into markers of His goodness. When I see clay jars, they remind me that He brought me through gut-wrenching pain a little more filled with His light, a little more prepared for what was around the bend. They remind me that it's His story that gets me home, not mine.

And for Elizabeth, it's the same way. When that big orange *T* flaps against her front door, it reminds her of a completely different kind of story, the one where a loving God called her out for His own and gave her *His* name, which is by far the best one of all.

It really does feel different when God gets in your heart and replaces your dreams with Himself. Our hearts become blank canvases where He can paint pictures of His love, fill us up with His Spirit, and change our desires and hurts from the inside out. It feels different. We begin to see Him write a new story. One with a whole lot of freedom.

WHAT'S THE "GOLD" IN YOUR LIFE? AND RIGHT NOW IS IT IN YOUR POCKET OR YOUR HEART?

_____

_____

_____

_____

_____

_____

_____

_____

seven

WHAT FREEDOM FEELS LIKE

I'd heard it said before, and it's true: *there's no real way to describe it*. And until you experience it for yourself, it's impossible to know what it feels like.

The top of the world is *cold*. Seriously. It's crazy cold up there.

To me, everything south of the freezing point had always looked the same in my head. Whether 30 degrees or -30, Alabama or Alaska, it was all big-coat, frozen-breath, don't-stand-outside-for-very-long cold. I'd seen videos of people in Siberia throwing cups of coffee in the air to watch them freeze instantly. I knew people up there wore what they wore for a reason.

But I couldn't comprehend that kind of cold. Winter weather had always been a one-size-fits-all kind of misery that a good layer of outerwear could shield you from, no matter the temperature. And that sentiment held until the day I jumped off a train in Estonia into knee-deep snow and everything got real, and it felt different.

I rode the overnight train into my friend Kelsey's icebox-of-a-life on Christmas Eve. She was moving from Russia to the really-far-up-there country of Estonia, a place that can only wring six hours of non-direct sunlight from the sky at the height of winter. It's kind of like the sun does a drive-by every day around noon to grab lunch and hurry home to spend the afternoon watching Netflix. It wasn't at all concerned about giving us a warm welcome. Kelsey had tried to prep me for that—and for our unconventional dismount from the train.

When the right moment came, we were going to have to throw all of Kelsey's earthly possessions from the back door of the caboose as we rolled through the little town she was moving to. It was a task for more than one set of hands, and since I was sort of nearby, I had happily agreed to be the extra set. I'd always needed an excuse to ride the Polar Express in real life—a Polar Express with less Tom Hanks and more Russian bag-sniffing hounds whose Christmas was made by finding a jar of American peanut butter in one of Kelsey's duffel bags.

It was a long night. The snow-dusted track from Moscow to Estonia seemed to never end. We could've used more hot chocolate, for sure. Well into the morning we dozed on the warm train until suddenly somebody yelled at us, and then it all happened so fast.

We were throwing bags off the caboose and jumping into the pillowy snow and watching the train pull away from us in the midmorning dawn. The train's wheels stopped for a generous several seconds, but since I didn't have any experience train hopping, it felt like they could've given us a little longer. But we made it. All the bags did too. We took a deep breath.

And as I sucked in the air, it stabbed me in the lungs. Cold. *Oh my gosh, cold.* It froze our faces. Our feet. Our hair. I'm not sure how my organs were faring, but it felt like the cold went all the way through my gut. I yelped like a Russian drug hound.

Kelsey laughed at me. "I told you it was gonna be—"

"I know. You did. I just couldn't even imagine."

There's no real way to describe it. *Until you experience it for yourself.* So this is it, friends. It's time. It's time to experience it. This is the moment where our feet find themselves standing at the back of the Russian train, gripping our bags in our hands, trying to figure out where to leap. Or how. Or when. Or if.

It's a heavy load we're holding on to. We've got the pain of desperately wanting things we don't have—things we don't have yet, things we may never have, things we lost and can't get back. We have the pain of feeling misunderstood in our hurt. We have the anxiety of not knowing what the rest of this blank slate is going to look like.

These bags are awfully heavy. Our tired arms strain to hold them here where we stand at the door. We ache from sharing our seats with them, contorting ourselves around them for miles and miles and miles. They've crowded our spaces. They've cramped our lives. And even now, standing here, they cramp our arms. Our backs. Our hearts.

We can tell stories all day.

WE CAN TALK ABOUT GALAXIES AND OCEANS AND A GOD WE COULD NEVER DREAM OF FITTING IN OUR POCKET.

We can talk about how our paths went rogue, our tissue piles got big, and our dreams were pick-pocketed like Skittles.

We can talk about the God who runs to us, love coursing through His veins, while we stand here in our hurt. Between us, we've got an awful lot of hurt. It's raw. We hate it. But we don't know what to do about it. Just standing here makes our souls tired. It's time to *do something*. And above the rhythmic, nonstop hum of the train on the tracks, the whisper comes again, *Look up. Freedom awaits.*

At this point, the old familiar words start ringing in our ears again. *Give it all to Jesus. Give Him everything.*

He's better than anything you could ever want here, better than anything you're holding on to. He really can be enough.

Our shoulders droop. And we think, *I've tried that. I've tried "giving it all to Jesus." I've tried meeting Him in the Word. I've tried prayer. I've tried telling God that He can have it all. I've tried it all. It didn't work. And I'm exhausted.*

But many of us who say those words haven't really opened our eyes and our hearts to realize that we're still standing there on the back of the train, bags in hand, toes dangling over the edge.

It feels similar to letting go. We still feel the brisk wind of the cold air moving around us, tickling our faces, chilling our breath. God is nearby. We see and feel Him around us. We're up out of our seats. We're poised to throw our bags off. We feel close enough to think we've done it. We think we've fully surrendered. It seems like the real deal.

But as we stand there, we labor to stay upright, swaying with the weight of the stuff we're holding. We wonder why this feels so hard, but we keep hanging in there with God and pushing through like champs. But the sensation of fresh air in our lungs pales in light of the load we feel pulling us down. If we're honest, we'll say it. *This doesn't feel like freedom. And I'm not sure how long I can keep this up.*

>>———→

It's hard to put words to what freedom actually feels like. But one thing's for sure. It's *light*. And it fills my friend Heather's house in Alabama.

As we sat and talked, colored bulbs twinkled on the overly fat Christmas tree, and pale winter sunlight danced across the kitchen table. The bulbs and tree and sunlight added to what was already there, a lightness that draws people in and pushes them toward Jesus.

It hasn't always been that way—Heather will be the first to say it. There were a lot of years when the push-pull to get adult life under control left her empty and out of step with God. But when it changed, everything changed. Night and day, she'd say.

Light reigns now. You can see it in her eyes. It's real. And now that she's felt it, she wants so badly for others to feel it too.

"How do you tell people what it feels like, real freedom in Christ?"

Heather sat back into the deep chair in deep thought, a look on her face like I'd asked the million-dollar question. "I can't. I can't explain it."

"Try."

She thought for a minute, smiled, and shrugged. "I can't. But what I *can* say is that if you don't feel it, it's because you're still holding on to something. And I *can* say that once you have it, you *know*. It's more real than anything you've ever felt. It's so radically different that nothing ever looks the same again."

Nothing.

Nothing ever looks the same again.

Not your happiness, not your hurt, not your hard days. Not your house or your family or your car or your job.

"It's just freedom, real freedom, to hand everything over to God," Heather said. "I'm not in control of my life, and it's a *good* thing. Good or bad, it's not in my hands. Neither way do I get the credit. It's not my life now—it's His. It takes the pressure off."

It takes the pressure off because we know Him and trust that everything is ultimately for our good.

WE TRUST HIS UNIVERSE-BUSTING LOVE FOR US, FOR EACH ONE OF US.

For you. For me.

"Now I look to Him for everything. I look to Him to use my life the way He wants to and to know what I need. I look to Him to show me how to make my heart more like His. I read His Word, and He fills me up with Himself to the point that it's not me anymore. Everything of me is on the table, and that's given Him room to fill me up with all of Him.

"And because I know it's Him, I trust that whatever happens isn't ruining my story—it's actually writing the story He wants to write. And that's the one that's filled with the most joy."

With God holding all the pieces of your life, joy becomes burst-your-heart full, because it's got nothing tethering it down. Pain can still be deep, but it feels radically different—a lot lighter. We hurt and grieve without the intense weight of having to figure out *why* or *what in the world are You doing, God?* or *how in the world is this going to work out well for me?*

The *why* falls off the back of the train. It dissipates in the wind of who He is and what He is working out in our hearts and in the bigger story. Do we still struggle? Of course. We're still living in these bodies of flesh, sinful cages that wage constant war against our soul. And the more of God we get, the more we realize just how weak we are. That's why He shines through the cracks in our vessels, why *His strength is made perfect in our weakness.* That's why we are told we have this treasure of His presence and love and salvation in our "jars of clay," our earthly tents, "to show that the surpassing power belongs to God and not to us" (2 Corinthians 4:7).

And that's not a bad thing, us realizing our frailty.

Nothing else spurs us to surrender and freedom like being reminded of how big, strong, and trustworthy He is in comparison to us.

"It's not up to me to figure anything out, and that's good. He's so much better at that than I am," Heather said. "It's not up to me to try to plan how anything is going to end up. I don't need a plan. I don't need a certain life. He's enough, and He's so much better than anything I could figure out on my own, and the moment I laid all those parts of my life on the table is the moment He became everything."

Everything. We need nothing else. We grasp at nothing else. We have all we need in Him. Our hearts are light. We have light in our eyes, in our empty hands. Him becoming our everything aligns our lives in the way they were created to be aligned. It creates order out of chaos. It changes how we view His worth and measure the worth of everything around us, which changes the way we treat everything in our lives, from big to small.

We value what's meant to be valued. We let everything else slip through our fingers like heavy bags dropped from the train. *And what we find in our hands in its place is infinite gain.* It really does change everything.

He's a cruel enemy, the one who cruises around our lives lulling us into thinking that standing in the ready position on the back of the train, bags in hand, is the same as giving God all we've got. *It's not. It's not the same.* And until we throw everything off and jump, we'll never understand why that is. The life that comes with jumping is kind of like the Baltic snow in Estonia—you can't understand how it feels until it hits your skin. It's indescribable. It's deep and light simultaneously. It kills and it brings to life at the same time. It's a living paradox. *It is the only way to live.* It requires everything, but it gives everything in return.

Jesus put it this way: "The kingdom of heaven is like treasure hidden in a field, which a man found and covered up. Then in his joy he goes and sells all that he has and buys that field" (Matthew 13:44). And there it is. There's the difference between standing and jumping. *It's all about our heart.* It's not just about whether or not you go and literally sell everything you own and give it away—though God may ask for that. In Scripture, sometimes Jesus asked that of people and sometimes He didn't. He knew their hearts, and He knew how to point a finger straight at where their treasures really lay.

Because "where your treasure is, there your heart will be also" (Matthew 6:21).

That's where real surrender comes in—positioning our hearts to hold everything loosely, to be willing to do anything He asks of us with total obedience and surrender. It's about the attitude with which we open our hands. This idea of standing at the back of the train wrestling our bags and yelling into the winter sky, *"Why, God? What do You ask of me? What do You want from me? What do I do?"*—it's not the way it's meant to be.

For real—how did we get there? How did we determine that this is the way we find freedom? I've done my share of angst-ridden "surrender," and it's just plain not in the Bible. What's there looks completely different.

Give up yourself and everything you have to follow Me, and I will call you sons and daughters and be with you forever in a place where you'll never shed another tear. There's story after story like this, where Jesus offers a light burden and asks for everything in return. The men and women who chose to take Him up on it did so with their eyes set on what they were *getting*, not on what they were *giving up*. They really saw Him, and they wanted Him alone. There was no wavering. It didn't feel like a sacrifice. Easy, no. But simple, yes.

SOMEHOW WE'VE MANAGED TO COMPLICATE IT, MANAGED TO MAKE IT AN ACT OF GUT-WRENCHING RESIGNATION AND SHEER WILL TO TURN OVER OUR LIVES AND DREAMS TO GOD.

It's like the money we slip into the offering plate while thinking of things we'd rather be spending it on—but we know this is right, so we're doing it and hoping God follows through with something good.

He knows we're inclined to do this. He lets us waver. He lets us question, doubt. He lets us struggle with the things we offer Him, take them back, hold them out again, take them back. He's patient in His love. But He wants us to be free. And when we finally jump, there's a marked difference—not in Him, but in us. That guy in Jesus' story about the field caught a glimpse of the treasure available to him, and *in his joy* he traded everything he had.

Joy. He gave his life to get the kingdom of God *out of sheer joy* about what he was getting. He was looking at it through an otherworldly set of eyes, a heart soaked in the truth of who God is, the truth of the reward waiting for us in the final pages of the Bible.

It's a taste, a joy we cultivate through knowing God. It's not our natural bent to crave that—we crave answers and the next step. But if we open our eyes and our hearts to see, and if we whet our passion for Him on the truth of His Word, He plants the desire in us and it grows more and more insatiable with time and prayer and staying in step with Him. That's the difference between Him and any other desire we have stirring in our hearts. *There's infinite fulfillment to be had.*

Elisabeth Elliot said we naturally cling to the things we love here, thinking that we will lose everything important if we let God tamper with it. We're like a tiny seashell, she said, full of a few drops of water but nervous to dump those drops out just in case there's not enough water in the ocean to fill us back up.

When I was standing there clutching everything that mattered to me in my hands, wondering if I could trust the God of the universe with my dreams, there wasn't much joy in the thought of giving them up. It felt more like frustration, or desperation, or hurt, or insecurity. Normal human emotions, for sure, but they showed me something deeper about my heart. I hadn't seen God yet for who He really is, for what He's really worth. If I had, I would've sold everything I owned to buy that field. I would've dropped everything else that had my heart. And I would've never looked back.

When it comes to unfulfilled dreams, figuring out how to create better, fuller lives for ourselves won't help. It might help a little and for a little while. But it won't heal the deep root issue.

A HEALTHY VIEW OF GOD IS THE ONLY THING THAT WILL.

That's why it's so important to know His Word, to know who He is, and who He says we are to Him. That's why it's so important to talk with Him, to ask Him to show Himself to us, to ask Him how to know Him better, to tell

Him what's going on in our hearts, and to ask Him to make Himself big to us.

That's why it's so important to spend time getting to know who God the Father is, a holy, all-consuming God who will bring justice on the earth one day, who will bring us in His great love to dwell with Him as daughters and sons in His Kingdom. That's why it's so important to know His Son, Jesus, the Lamb of God who takes away the sins of the world, the God in flesh who dwelt among us and asked us to leave houses and mothers and brothers to follow Him. The One who said, "Trust Me. It's worth it."

That's why it's so important to know the Spirit, the One who whispers to us even now in our hearts and through the truth of God's Word that there's more to life than what we can see right in front of us. There's so much more.

Let go.

When we see the fullness of God's glory and the fullness of His love radiating through Scripture, the vastness of who He is and how trustworthy He has been since before the beginning of time, we know we can trust Him. We haven't been forgotten. We haven't been overlooked. We haven't been mistreated. We've simply been loved overwhelmingly by a God who can write our stories much better than we can—for our good. And when we know Him and we see the story He's already written, we know we're in good hands.

It's then that we know we can jump with abandon like little children to a Father who's got His arms up, waiting to catch us. And we realize not only that we *can*, but we *want to*—with joy. At that point, all our dreams become things not to cling to and yell *why* over but to throw off as quickly as possible, the dead weight that's keeping us from getting there faster.

Because when our eyes see Him, *really see Him*, everything else pales. We want Him. More than anything, we want Him, and we want Him to do whatever it takes to order our lives in such a way that we know Him more. It's not a checklist or a reluctant sacrifice—it's pure desire.

That's what He wants. He doesn't want our performance. He doesn't want our resigned decision, like we're going through with an arranged marriage we feel we're not allowed to back out of. He wants our whole heart. And when we see Him for who He is, we want to give it. We throw the bags off the train without a second thought. It's the end of ourselves.

IT'S THE BEGINNING OF REAL LIFE.

We jump. We feel the freedom on our skin, in our hearts.

So, friend, the question comes to you. Maybe it's not the question you're used to considering. It's not: *Do you trust Him?*—though that's vital. It's not: *Are you willing to give Him everything?*—though that's crucial too. It's simply this: *When you think about giving God all of yourself, everything you have, everything you've ever dreamed of, what stirs in your heart? Is it joy?* Because if it isn't, this whole thing isn't going to work. God hasn't become big enough to be worth it yet, and obedience to Him is going to be nothing short of exhausting.

This process has no time line, no amount of time it has to take for God to become big in your heart. Paul, a full-on persecutor of Christians, saw Jesus on the road to Damascus one day, and one real glimpse was all it took for him to radically give up everything he'd ever known in exchange for life with God. Formerly a respected leader, he spent the rest of his life enduring persecution, such as being in prison, snake-bitten, hungry, shipwrecked, and beaten. And he said he had learned to be content in every situation. He counted it all *joy.*

I have friends with stories a little bit like Paul's. For others, the process is slower, a gradual revelation leading to the moment the scales fall off and they see Him as real and worth everything, the ultimate prize. My experience was more like that. But either way, you have to get there, or you'll never stop holding all your heavy bags. They'll go with you for the rest of your life, and over every mile you'll wonder why God never did anything about it, why He never brought you any relief. *And freedom was waiting all along.*

In those moments of silence when you really delve into what's in your heart, what do you see? What desires are there that are still unmet? A spouse? Children? A different kind of job? A different kind of family? A different kind of life? Lay them out. Think about them. Take a good, long look at what's there. And ask yourself this: *If He never fulfilled that desire, would I be able to be content? If I walk a road where those things never happen, would I be filled with joy knowing I would get Him at the end?*

If the answer is no, I dare you to ask yourself another question: *Why does God seem smaller in my heart than this life I want?* I dare you to ask Him this question: *God, would You please show me who You really are?*

I DARE YOU TO SIT IN THE SILENCE AND LOOK FOR HIM, NOT FOR ANSWERS TO THOSE HEAVY *WHYS*, BUT JUST TO KNOW HIM.

I dare you to talk to Him, not about the things that you want, but about how you want to know Him. I dare you to read about Him, to study His Word, to ask for more and more of the reality of who He is to sink into your heart. I dare you to put that above everything else.

Our hearts are key. We have to want Him for Him, not

for relief. We have to want everything He is and everything He offers us. We have to find that pursuit *pure joy*. And if we do, He will meet us there with love, light, peace, and freedom. He says if we seek Him with all of our heart, we will find Him. So it's time, friends. It's time for things to be different. It's time to stop settling for angst when freedom awaits. It's time to realize that nothing we will ever have can hold a candle to God and His eternal love and glory.

It's time to know Him while He can be known. Don't rest until you do.

WHAT THINGS ARE YOU HOLDING ON TO THAT ARE KEEPING YOU FROM REAL FREEDOM?_____

_____

_____

_____

_____

_____

_____

_____

_____

_____

part two

WHEN FREEDOM WRITES OUR STORIES

*These all died in faith, not having received the
things promised, but having seen them and greeted
them from afar, and having acknowledged that
they were strangers and exiles on the earth. . . .
They desire a better country, that is, a heavenly
one. Therefore God is not ashamed to be called
their God, for he has prepared for them a city.*

—Hebrews 11:13, 16

eight

IT ONLY GETS BETTER FROM HERE

The fields just kept going. And going and going and going. They stretched out wide and flat and golden as far as you could see in every direction. The spindly arms of hundreds of modern windmills—to me the creepiest-looking things on the planet—lazily lapped at the breezes blowing across the plains.

Five hours on I–70, and the scenery never changed. Not once. Apparently, this was Kansas and everything Kansas was famous for. It almost seems like a cruel joke for the endless plains to sit right next to a state that scored a lifelong marriage to the Rocky Mountains. You cruise out of Denver with the snowcapped peaks in your rearview mirror, and as they fade away, you begin to question everything you know to be good in this world. At the state line, the sign reads, "Leaving Colorful Colorado," not so subtly implying that, congratulations, you might never see color again for the rest of your life. It doesn't really seem fair. In fact, it's famously unfair.

As I stopped to stretch my legs at a rest stop that was a gas station and Starbucks in one—advertised on billboards as the "Oasis of the Plains"—I received a message from Amy B, a text superimposed over a photo of a field just like the ones I'd been staring at for hours.

"Welcome to Kansas, destroying people's will to live since 1861."

I laughed. But I'll admit—though they are never-ending, the fields are pretty. Really pretty. The sun and the breeze have definitely figured out how to make this place their playground. The sky is huge and blue here, and the light dances on the wind-whipped wheat. It's the heart of America, and America has a big heart of gold.

That night just as the sun was starting to set, the scenery broke, and suddenly there was Wichita. I pulled into the bed-and-breakfast where I'd booked a room for the night, and it wasn't long before a roaring fire in the fireplace made Kansas look even better.

"How was your drive?"

"It was great," I told the house owners, and I was being truthful. The lazy, golden wallpaper that had made me want to hum Aaron Copland tunes for five hours straight had been the perfect backdrop for a lot of good phone conversations and thinking time.

"Kansas has some beautiful scenery," I said.

You should've seen their faces—they held an authentic mix of delight, gratitude, and relief, as if I were the first one who'd ever told them their ugly baby was cute. I felt for them. It seemed like they were victims of a cruel marketing mishap. That's unfortunate. Because that night with the fire dancing in the hearth and wheat fields dancing in my head, I was perfectly fine to stay. It may not look like Colorado, but there's a lot of really full life here. And there are a lot of people who miss it because they have the accelerator to the floor.

It happens with Kansas, and it happens with what's considered slightly out-of-the-ordinary paths in life, the ones that don't have the same scenery and obvious markers of passing time. Like when you're single or childless past the age when everyone else thinks you should build a family. Or when you've stalled out in your career and are choosing to go back to school and start over, or try something new altogether.

Oh no. You're going to have to drive through the wastelands, huh? Hope it doesn't last too long.

Even if they—or we—don't say it out loud, often there's a sense that whatever we're getting into is not going to be nearly as good as what could've been if we'd been able to live in the mountains instead. Like we're going to live a life with less color. A life with *less*, period.

I'm sure you can find a way to make the best of it. It's not what you wanted, but I'm sure there's a way to make it okay.

It doesn't have to be like that. As you crank up the car, slip a different word in your pocket for the journey. This path you're on isn't meant to make you lose the will to live. It isn't meant to see if you can survive the subpar life and make lemonade when life hands you lemons. It's meant to write the best ending to your story. And not the best possible ending you can get with the available resources at this point in the game. *The best.* Period. Better than you could've ever written for yourself.

The wooden spoons that were laid across the pots split the clouds of steam in half as they rose from the bubbling low-country boil that Heather had on the stove for dinner. Potatoes. Corn. Meat. All simmering away separately. Ryan, Heather's seven-year-old foster son, juggled his plate excitedly as we prepared to dish up. This was one of his favorite meals.

But when Amy H and I got our food and sat down at the kitchen table, we noticed Ryan's plate and smiled—it was a mound of shrimp. Couldn't blame him for trying.

"Ryan, go get some of the other stuff too. Then if you're still hungry, you can have some more shrimp."

"Okay, Mom."

I watched Heather out of the corner of my eye. She wasn't "Mom" the last time I'd seen her . . . which was only eight months ago. Now her two-bedroom apartment was filled with toys, her refrigerator papered with spelling tests and artwork. Her potted plant was still swaying a bit from being hit by a soccer ball right before dinner. She was a little kid's mom. *Weird*. We had a lot to talk about.

After dinner, the three adults sat in the living room sipping tea and catching up, and the tenderhearted kid wandered in and out of our serious conversation.

WE TOLD STORIES OF WHERE GOD HAD BROUGHT US THAT YEAR, AND WE RELIVED HIS FAITHFULNESS.

He had pieced our paths together in a way we never could've imagined through the seeming wastelands of failed dreams and changed plans.

"It doesn't look anything like I thought it would," I said.

Amy laughed. "Yeah, I definitely didn't picture it going this way when I was younger." She was lined up to have a little girl placed with her through the foster system any day now.

"Is Amy's little girl going to be your girlfriend?" Heather teased Ryan.

He made a face and shook his head emphatically. Too young to keep his options open. As he came in and out from playing in the other room, Heather answered his questions. He did a toothbrush dance for us—the one he does when he and Heather brush their teeth before bed. At one point in the evening, he finally cocked his head to one side and asked, "Is this a Bible study?"

He crawled up in Heather's lap, and she said, "No, it's not a Bible study. It's just friends talking. When God is your life, you talk about Him all the time."

Ryan wrapped his arms around her neck and thought about that for a second. He was no stranger to this topic—Heather had been telling him about God ever since he moved in with her.

He fixed his eyes on me across the room and said, "Grace, how do you know God?"

Wow, Father. Look what You're doing here. Look at the story You're writing in the midst of what might seem to be a less-than-ideal situation.

Thanks to the groundwork Heather had been laying, I got to tell that little kid about how God had spoken to me through a Bible verse when kids were picking on me on the playground when I was about his age. How I'd known then that He wasn't just stories or a big God up there just doing His thing—that He loved me and spoke to me personally. And that as the years went on, I realized more and more how important it was for me to really know Him.

He asked Amy and Heather the same question, and they told their stories too.

"My parents taught me about God, and then I got to know Him better by talking to Him and reading about Him. I've known Him a long time now. We're tight, like peanut butter and jelly," Heather said, crossing her fingers.

Ryan grinned.

"I know His voice," she said. "I don't hear it like I hear yours, but I hear it in my heart because I've talked to Him and listened to Him for so long." She poked Ryan in the stomach playfully. "What about you? What's *your* story? How do *you* know God?"

"I moved in with you, and then you taught me," he said.

Heather hugged him. "Your story's still happening, isn't it?"

I caught her gaze.

"All of ours are, aren't they?"

I imagine if you asked Heather, she'd say she never would've imagined her story looking like this. She'd been in serious relationships before. And she'd had a pretty different story in mind, one that had her living overseas. She never would've imagined that "single foster mom at thirty-four" would be woven into her story.

She's tired. You can see it in her face. But far bigger than the tired is the light that pours from her eyes, a spark that ignited when a blunt friend challenged her to get serious or get out, to stop playing around with following Jesus. She snapped awake. She chose the first option.

And she met with Him. Read about His love. Saw it for herself. Told Him she wanted nothing else. The result of that was a heart sold out, a bond unbreakable. Like peanut butter and jelly. And the result of *that* was that a little boy got a home.

This was her Kansas, but it didn't feel like everyone had told her it would—it was actually really beautiful.

IT WASN'T HER WASTELAND; IT WAS HER STORY, AND IT WAS HAPPENING ON PURPOSE, BEING WRITTEN BY A LOVING GOD.

She didn't become a foster mom to fill a gap. She became a foster mom because the gap had already been filled. When Heather laid down her own dreams, Jesus rushed into her life in a way that overhauled her heart and filled in all the cracks. He became the only thing that mattered. His Word became her life.

"The Bible isn't to give me warm, fuzzy feelings; it's to lead me to God," I remember her telling us one night. "You can't fall in love with someone you don't know."

As she fell in love with Him, her desire for Him and

His story quickened, and He began to awaken new desires in her. A desire to help others to know the same peace she did. A desire to care for children who don't have parents.

"It's messy," she said with a smile. "But it's better than I could've ever come up with on my own."

When it happens—when we become like peanut butter and jelly with the God of the universe—there's really no limit to how deep, how rich our story can be. All bets are off as to what He will do when we give Him everything in order to know His presence in our lives.

HIS LOVE MEETS OUR WHOLEHEARTED OBEDIENCE, AND OUR STORIES START TO SING.

And something changes in our hearts too. We don't see our journey like a wasteland anymore. We see it as Plan A. Every step has purpose, because we're headed toward Him. And that strips away the weight we feel to figure out *what* or *why* and replaces it with peace and freedom. We start to look forward with joy—not because we're waiting on something earthly, but because we know what God has around the bend for us is more of Himself.

It only gets better. Even now, just thinking about it, I feel a smile slipping across my face. I'll be honest. I'm in my thirties, and I have no idea what the rest of my life is going to look like. I don't even know what this year is going to look like. Sometimes I feel like I'm living in some sort of timeless state while my peers rack up years of marriage and their kids work their way through elementary and middle school. I feel a little like my path has gone rogue.

But even though the "normal" markers—like wedding anniversaries or children's birthdays—just aren't there, these years have had markers of their own, ones that to me personally mean more than the "normal" ones ever could. They're spiritual markers, markers between God and me. They fill journal after journal, corner after corner of my heart. They're places and times and ways I've seen God. *Really seen Him.* And they're worth all my gold, all my dreams.

They're a testimony to the story of how He's become everything to me—and how I want still more of Him. The stories these markers represent aren't all easy. But the best stories never have been easy.

The story that landed me on a big green hill in England was one of those not-so-easy stories. But for the most unexpected reasons, it became one of my favorites. That hill became one of my favorites too. On days when the British clouds broke, I'd sit there and watch the tiny trains move across the miniature town down in the valley. I felt as though I were watching a way more picturesque version of the toy engine that used to wrap around the ceiling of the Dairy Queen in my college town, chugging by a scene painted on the top eight inches of the walls. What a horribly unworthy comparison. This place was crazy beautiful, and there was no soft serve in sight.

Is this real life? Can't be. That town down there—that was my town. And if that tiny train hadn't been in motion, I'd have thought the whole scene was a painting. This was countryside England, big and green and gorgeous. Every single building there was pretty. Old and pretty. Forget hastily built subdivisions. Forget strip malls. Things were built to last. Pretty much every tiny building on the horizon looked like it had been created by Jane Austen's pen, even the bike shop and the grocery store and the Starbucks, which all sat on a main street that wrapped around a clock tower and castle grounds.

Every single day for two whole years, I felt like I should slap myself. I couldn't believe I got to live there. But it was a difficult good-bye that christened my move to England. Rewind the clock to a few months before the plane brought me here, and you'll find me in a different park saying a different kind of good-bye—to the first guy who was part of my life in a significant way since I'd watched that other relationship disintegrate years before. This time, I was sitting on a park bench, smiling through watery eyes as we both said we believed God knew what He was doing in ending the relationship we'd been pursuing, that God had our good in mind. I meant it. But I thought I might never understand why he'd had to come my way in the first place. In that moment, it sure didn't feel great.

I'd been single for several years at that point. And in that span of time, God had drawn me to the back of the figurative train to get a glimpse of who He really was, throw all my desires into His waiting arms, jump into His love, and experience the full freedom of following Him. For the first time in several years, single felt not just livable but good. Really, really good.

"Jumping" had let me turn loose of all the unmet desires that had been eating up space in my heart and freed me to follow God with abandon, to want nothing but His love.

IT FREED MY HEART UP TO LONG FOR ALL GOD HAS TO OFFER, TO BE FILLED WITH HIS LOVE FOR THE LOST AND THE HURTING.

It freed me up to really *live*.

Suddenly, a really great guy walked into my life with

a heart for all the same things. We began to talk. And talk more. And as we did, over a span of months, we grew to respect each other even more. It was great.

It was horribly timed.

I was in the middle of preparing to move to England to start a new job there. And neither of us knew what to do with that. I didn't have peace about staying—I knew God had been clear in saying it was time to go. For a while, I thought we might try to keep pursuing something while I was away, but that was starting to sound more and more complicated. Finally, he was the one to say it: *This just isn't the right thing or the right timing.*

He was right. But gosh, it hurt. I remember sitting on the tan carpet in my living room later that day, telling God I trusted Him even though I didn't understand.

God, a few months ago, I was just cruising along, living my life, perfectly fine with it being just me and You. That was simple. I don't understand why this had to come along right now, right in the middle of getting ready to move, just for my heart to get hurt. It doesn't make any sense.

It felt like needless distraction. Needless pain. And it compounded the raw hurt I was already feeling about leaving behind family and friends and closing the Alabama chapter of my life, a chapter I really, really loved. *But even so, I trust You.* As I sat there talking to God with my Bible open, I found myself in the book of Job, reading the words

Job spoke when he suffered much, much grander loss: "Though he slay me, I will hope in him" (Job 13:15).

When Job found out all of his children had died, his whole livelihood had been swept away, he wept. But he also fell on the ground and worshipped. "That's what I want to do too, God," I whispered. "From the big losses to the small, I want to say like Job, 'The LORD gave, and the LORD has taken away; blessed be the name of the LORD'" (Job 1:21).

In that moment, I heard Him whisper to my heart, *You've said that you've given Me everything, that you want Me to do whatever it takes for you to really know Me. What if it's going to take going through some pain to really know Me?*

I knew in that instant that He was right. I'd told Him that He could have everything I had, even my life, but I hadn't given Him permission to use hard things to shape me, things that hit really close to my heart.

I'D MADE THAT OFF LIMITS, AND I DIDN'T EVEN REALIZE IT.

I didn't realize I'd been holding something back, but I'd been praying for Him to show me if I was.

I fell on my face. *You can have that too, God. You can have that too.*

A few months later, I found myself sitting on that big green hill near my new house in England with a crazy, jet-lagged look in my eye. I didn't even know where to buy groceries. Or scissors. Or pillows. This was crazy. But it was *awesome*. I mean, have you *seen* this place?

A grin crept across my face. "Father, I know You brought me here," I whispered. "I can't wait to see what You're going to do."

The year before, when I'd finally reached the point of full surrender, I found myself on my face at the foot of the cross—literally. I'd been working behind the scenes at a conference, and suddenly in the middle of doing my job, it hit me. Everything I'd seen of God in His Word over the months prior erupted to the top of my heart. And I knew it—I hadn't really given Him everything. There were some things, some dreams I was still holding back for myself. And it was like I couldn't put my stuff down fast enough, get out the door fast enough to find some place to get by myself and tell Him. *God, You can have it all.*

Funny enough, the closest place was a prayer room, a prayer room with a huge cross at the back of it. It could have been any room at that point, it didn't matter. But that cross definitely gave a visual to that moment I'll never forget.

God, You can have everything. I hold nothing back. I keep none of my own desires for my life. I only want You. I'll go anywhere. I'll do anything. I'll give up anything. Just please write the story You want with my life, the one that has You at the end of it.

That was the moment I felt the bags fly out of my

hands and off the back of the train. And I jumped. That was the moment my growing desire for God and my obedience intersected. *Deny yourself, take up your cross daily, and follow Me.* For the first time, I began to feel in my heart what that really meant. I began to feel it daily. The implications are different every day, and they're different for each person. Following Jesus is not just doing something. But it's also not just feeling something. It's both.

It's what God tells you to do in that place where His love for you and your love for Him intersect with wholehearted obedience. And on that day, for me, to *follow* meant to *go*. It meant that I laid down all the things I loved about my life—my job, my friends, my church, the outdoorsy things I liked to do, the close proximity to my family, a growing relationship with a guy—to say, *Whatever You want, God. I only want You.*

I LAID DOWN ALL THE THINGS I WANTED FOR THE FUTURE AND HANDED HIM A BLANK PAGE TO WRITE MY STORY.

I handed Him a blank check to spend my life however He wanted, as my pastor in Alabama likes to say.

God met me there. Nothing has felt the same since then. *Nothing.* Ever since then, I don't feel like God is helping me cope with unmet desires—I feel like He's given me bigger desires, new ones that overshadow the old ones so much that I don't even feel them much anymore. He's given me *joy*. I just want to know Him. And I want so much to help others know Him.

When I handed Him a blank piece of paper that day and He put His pen to it, He began to write an amazing story, one that redeemed the mistakes I'd made in the past, one that brought good even out of my sin and brokenness and the selfish way I'd lived. The years that followed have been the best years of my life. It was like He popped a new set of eyes in my head. I began to see things, see people more like the way He saw them. I couldn't get enough. Even the hard things pointed me back to Him, and I praised Him for that.

I treasure the years when England was my home. It was the backdrop against which God's story in my life began to get rich and full and He began to be my every breath. I treasure my time there. I treasure the friends I made there. I treasure the way I saw God move, the people I saw Him draw to Himself, the way He drew me to Himself.

There were still some really hard things to come. And that almost-relationship had also set in motion another plot twist I didn't know about yet, one that would see me leave England way earlier than I'd planned. Heartbreaking good-byes would christen that move too.

But there's no way in a million years I'd trade what God did in that season for any kind of different life. Not a husband. Not kids. Not anyone else's story. *Because this is the story You wrote for me. I'm seeing Your hand all over it, and I know it leads me to You. And that is the sweetest truth my heart has ever known.*

Sometimes I wish I knew how to describe it better, the feeling of God invading your life and rewriting your heart's desires. But I find that the people who do describe it best do so without words. Like the subject of a video Heather sent me recently.

Did you see it? she wrote a few minutes after I'd received the text.

Yeah, I texted back. *I just watched it.*

No, Heather wrote, *I mean, did you see that guy?*

I mean . . . of course I saw him. The whole video that she'd sent me was about him. *He had no arms or legs.* And he was living a really full life.

Yeah, that's amazing, I wrote.

It was. He is roughly our age and was born with no limbs, and I think it goes without saying, that sets you up for a life pretty different from what's considered the "normal" kind of good. It's a wilderness, by all popular definitions. And for all his young years, he said he wondered why God had forgotten him, why He'd given him less. But in recent years, he found freedom in knowing that his life here is about knowing Christ and living exactly the story God created for him.

That changed his wilderness into something wonderful. He travels around telling his story, about how Christ is sufficient—and about how that makes his life *good*.

What attracted me to the video was that, of course, he has no arms and legs, Heather wrote. *But what was stranger was the freedom you could see smashed across his face and the peace of God flowing out of this guy's eyeballs. He has fully surrendered everything he has to Jesus, and God is using his life in mighty ways.*

In the video, he said he asked God why, and God said, *Do you trust Me?* When you answer *yes* to that question, nothing else matters. "Peace washes over you," he said. Since then, he has seen thousands upon thousands of people come to have light in their eyes because of the story God wrote for him.

The craziest thing I heard him say is, "I don't pray for arms and legs anymore. I don't want them," Heather wrote.

THAT'S A LOT MORE THAN HAVING GOD SUSTAIN YOU THROUGH DAYS AND WEEKS OF YOUR PRIMARY DESIRES BEING UNMET.

That's having new desires overshadow the old to the point that they don't run your life anymore. When that happens, Heather's right—peace flows out of your eyeballs.

"There is an unbelievable rush, higher than any drug or skydiving experience, that washes a peace that surpasses all understanding over every inch of my life when I lay down the things that I want," Heather said. "I've never heard anyone I know—or don't know, for that matter—describe anything that sounds better."

I never have either. *It's living in pure freedom.*

IT'S THE RUSH OF GOD WRITING A STORY WHERE WE SEE HIM AT EVERY TURN AND WAIT WITH ANTICIPATION TO SEE MORE.

So when I look forward to the coming year, and the year after that, and the year after that, I don't wonder anymore whether this will be the year that brings something different, like a husband, or a home, or something else along those lines. I wonder instead how I'm going to see God this year. That's what I pray for. *God, let me see You this year, let me know You more by the end of this year than I do at the beginning of it.*

Every year He's done far more than I can ask or think. There have been amazing blessings. There have been some really, really hard things. But in each and every moment, He's brought more of Himself, and He's brought it in ways that I never could've imagined or even thought to ask for. He can do that for you too. In fact, He *will*, if that's your all-out desire. He promises . . . *you'll seek Me and find Me, if you seek Me with all your heart.* And finding Him—more and more of Him all the time—drives us to ask for even more. It drives our story.

It's a good thing it drives it, because honestly, I don't even know what to ask for anymore. My story's gone so rogue that I don't even know what God *might* have in store next. But it's always better than I could have planned. So I request . . . *more of You, God. Whatever that means. Whatever needs to happen.*

IS IT HARD TO IMAGINE THAT THE STORY GOD HAS FOR YOU MIGHT ACTUALLY BE BETTER THAN THE ONE YOU WANT FOR YOURSELF?

_____

_____

_____

_____

_____

_____

_____

_____

nine

WHEN OUR MESS MEETS HIS MERCY

We lay on our backs in the thick grass, heads cushioned by our folded-up hoodies, toes kicking tiny pieces of chalky gravel over the edge of the mammoth cliff. Nothing like nap time right on the edge of death. What seemed like miles below us, the bright blue waves of the English Channel caught the white rocks as they fell soundlessly. Between the bigness of the wind, the water, and the cliffs, you never could tell when the gravel disappeared. Everything seemed small from that height.

My friend Clare and I lay there for a long time talking about boys. Life. God. What seemed like miles above us, the wind whipped two layers of clouds over each other in opposite directions.

"That's so weird looking," I said. "I wonder how far the white layer is above the gray layer."

"Oh, the gray layer is definitely the higher one. Definitely," Clare said, playfully picking a fight.

Never let a Brit entice you into a weather debate. You won't win. At least ten minutes passed with each of us thinking we were the one who knew what was going on, each of us saying different versions of "But see there? Look there. It's clearly moving underneath the other."

I'm still convinced she was wrong. But in the end, there was no way to know. Some things only God can see clearly. Things like what's really happening when it feels like the earth is giving way underneath us, crashing soundlessly into the sea below. Like it did when Clare died suddenly a few months later.

I didn't see it coming. No one did. It felt all out of order, all wrong. It was like getting punched in the gut, the air sucked from my lungs. Pain turned to hot lead in my chest.

HEARTS WEREN'T CREATED TO HAVE TO BREAK LIKE THAT. OR TO STAY BROKEN.

I thought a lot over the days and months that followed. *Why? Why her? Why now?* And most of all—*How can this be good?*

"That first time you face an obstacle—it hits you really hard." My nephew Ben stirred his drink with his straw. "I mean, when you think about it, all of us in our family lived pretty easy lives. Nothing really hard ever happened."

He was right. Growing up had been pretty easy. Things made sense. But it didn't stay that way. We graduated out into the real world and saw our perfect plans get crushed like chalky gravel under our toes. I found myself figuring out long-term equilibrium as a single adult. I lost my friend to a mysterious illness and found myself swimming in gut-crushing grief.

Our family had their share of boat-rocking tough times too. At twenty-nine, my niece Sara had already lost two of her closest friends to cancer. A year younger than her, her sister Jess has seen roadblock after roadblock in the path to the one thing she thought God was calling her to since childhood.

And Ben, their older brother, met obstacles along his path to the medical career he'd always dreamed of, obstacles that shocked him and shook him to his core. He'd always succeeded academically, even soared to the top of his class in med school, and in the final stretch, he took some exams that should've been no problem. But for the life of him, he couldn't pass them. It seemed like everything he'd ever planned was wrecked.

"I wondered why God would do this to me," he said. "When that first hard thing happens, when something gets taken away, or when things don't go the way you thought they would, when you don't understand why—that's when you really come face-to-face with whether or not you trust that God is good in your life, that what He's doing is good."

THE STORM LOOKS DIFFERENT FOR ALL OF US, BUT IT ALWAYS COMES.

It's not a question of "if" but "when" and "what." Rarely are we ready. People we love leave. They die. Houses burn down. Lives unravel. Parents get divorced. Chemo doesn't work. Women yearning to be mothers pass into menopause with empty houses. The things we always wanted for our lives never happen. And the things we never wanted do.

Our souls reject it. We all hurt—and hurt deeply at times. We all have questions. He can handle it—our hurt, our screaming, our broken pieces. But the ultimate bent of our broken hearts—peace or bitterness—comes down to this: *How big is God to us? How well do we know Him? And do we know Him well enough to trust that He's writing a better story than what we could've written ourselves?*

I'll never forget the way it felt to watch those four boys hoist that wicker casket onto their shoulders and turn to face a church packed full of Clare's family and friends. I'll never forget the look in his eyes, the boy holding the front left corner, the boy Clare had been talking to me about that day as we lay there on the cliffs.

Everything in me collapsed. My friends Bex and Mandi held me up on either side as we wept. And in the pain, my heart cried again . . . *how can this be good?* But as they walked down the aisle, the band began to play, and the well-known song that would jolt me to tears for years to come began to fall from my lips as I gasped for air.

The song declared that my heart had ten thousand reasons to praise Him, no matter what came, and no matter what was still to come. It hurt. But it was true. And my heart spilled out the words.

Losing Clare wasn't the story I was expecting God to write. I could've come up with a bunch of endings I thought were much, much better. Clare was one of the most vibrant people I've ever met, and when she met Jesus, it was like fireworks. She lit up whole rooms wherever she went.

SHE WANTED NOTHING MORE THAN TO KNOW HIS LOVE AND FOR EVERYONE ELSE TO KNOW IT TOO.

Her whole life was aimed at that—as she put it, she was "striving and hungry" for Him.

That packed church was a tiny snapshot of the impact that the light in her eyes had made on others. So what in the world was the benefit of taking this firecracker of a twenty-four-year-old out of southern England when who knows what she could've done for Him in forty or fifty more years on earth? *How was this better? How was this better for her family, her friends, the people she had yet to meet?*

It's messy, really messy, this place where our fragile human emotions and even frailer ability to comprehend the big picture meet the story of a God who touches our broken world with a love that doesn't make any sense. It's messy, the place where we look at our deep hurt and feebly remind our hearts that "we know that for those who love God all things work together for good, for those who are called according to his purpose" (Romans 8:28).

In this place, we tend to go to God like He's an equation. We think if what He's said is true, we should be able to make it all work out prettily if we put our pencils to paper and do the math right. It's tempting to want to point to that verse about how *all things work together for our good*, put Clare's death on one side of the equation and write "equals good" . . . and then get hurt. *Good? Seriously? How? Show me. Prove it.*

But like pretty much everything else in God's economy,

it's not an equation we can wrap our minds around. It's not
a + b = c.

IT'S A STORY WITH BILLIONS OF MOVING PARTS—THE INCALCULABLE PRODUCTS OF A BROKEN, SINFUL WORLD SLAMMING UP AGAINST THE INFINITE MERCY OF GOD.

And it's drawing one big, messy, beautiful picture. We
know God wins, and because He wins, so do we. But right
now the carnage is ferocious. It hurts. In our limited view it
looks like nothing adds up. It's hard to see that all is going
to end well.

I couldn't see much in front of me at all on a different day
a couple of years later in the Netherlands, just Dana's feet
wriggling and then disappearing through the hole in the
wall up ahead. I don't think she could've thrown her bag on
the floor any faster than she did when the tour guide asked
if anyone would like to crawl through the space under the
bottom shelf of the bookcase. Of course we would. I followed her feet. Just like that, we were standing in the tiny
space behind the wall, just big enough for a few people to
stand inside comfortably. I'd heard about this place since I
was a little girl. Corrie ten Boom's hiding place.

Corrie—a Dutch woman who never married—was in her fifties when she was sent to a Nazi concentration camp for hiding Jews during the Holocaust. She and her family saved hundreds of lives—including the six she hid in the secret room where Dana and I were standing. Her actions came at a high price. Corrie's father died after being arrested. Her sister, Betsie, died later in the concentration camp. And the women saw needless atrocities. Horrors. Death. Murder. Pain and starvation and disease and abuse and separation.

Why did any of that have to happen? Why did so many die? Why did Betsie? It wasn't long after Betsie's death that Corrie was released. They're questions we can't answer, questions that go back to the deep issue: *Is God really good? How in the world can this have a purpose? How can it end well?* They're questions Corrie herself may have asked. We know she wrestled through the horrors taking place around her, the personal grief that dug deep into her heart. But Betsie had these words for Corrie right in the midst of a horrific, deadly mess: "There is no pit so deep that [God] is not deeper still." And in that deep place, God was weaving wonders from the mess.

In the ten Boom house, a couple of floors below the hiding place, an embroidered gold crown hung beside the door in a small wooden frame. There wasn't anything flashy about it, but the stitching was hand sewn and exquisite. The tour guide reached past Dana and me, pulled the frame from the wall, and turned it over. The back was a straight-up mess. If you've ever done any stitching, you know what the underside of something like that looks like—an ugly tangle of threads with no visible picture at all.

That's the side we see, Corrie would say. In our pride, when He weaves the dark threads in with the bright ones, we forget that He can see the upper side—the real picture, the intricate design—while all we see is the mess.

"EVERY THREAD IS IMPORTANT," CORRIE SAID.

The happy ones. The easy years. The grief. The hard times. The lives saved. The things lost. "He knows, He loves, He cares," she wrote. "Nothing this truth can dim. He gives the very best to those who leave the choice to Him."

The best stories are always still ahead of us. And the hard moments are preparing us for them. That's the way the kingdom of God works. But what He knows is best might not be immediately visible. He's got an entirely different story in mind than we do. More than He wants us to experience the American dream for seventy years or so, He wants us to experience perfect joy for eternity. So He's more concerned about giving us what we need here to be able to get there and say, "In Christ, I've overcome the world." He's more concerned with our being able to say we are content in every circumstance because He is everything we need. He's more concerned with helping us know Him better *here* so that we're ready for *there*. Because *there* is worth it. *He* is worth it.

That's why Jesus told the rich guy to sell everything he owned—the stuff his life was wrapped up in—and give it to the poor so that he could know God. That's why Jesus said the kingdom of God belongs to little children, who love with abandon and don't hold anything back. That's why He said to store up our treasures in heaven rather than down here. Because Jesus *has seen and known the Father*— the Father who will dwell with us in the place where our real lives are going to be lived out for billions and billions of years. Jesus says it's worth it.

THE GOD WHO IS BIGGER THAN THE UNIVERSE IS WORTH IT.

When we think of Him that way, it takes heaven out of the dusty box on the shelf where we've put it. It wakes up the sleepy concept we've filed in our brains as the place we'll go one day after we get done with everything we want to do here. It brings eternity close and alive in a way that alters our present reality. It energizes the present. We start to see the lines blur between here and there. It makes our joy alive because we see it as a foretaste of what's to come. It brings eternal perspective to the moments we groan in pain because we know we are sharing in Christ's suffering and being made more like Him.

The truth we tell ourselves every day about God does affect our lives, as does what we tell ourselves about the things we hold most dear here on earth. It matters how we think about those things. It matters how we think about Him. And thinking about Him the right way starts with what He tells us about Himself through His Word, through the words we drink in every morning.

Like how much He loves us. How much He wants us to love Him back with everything we have. And how He's the prize worth having at any cost. That's why I prayed what I did at the beginning of the year when Clare died. *More of You, God. Whatever that means.*

When she died, it felt like a twenty-five-pound block of pain lodged in my abdomen, like I'd caught a cannon-ball with my gut. And in the days that followed, I couldn't pray. I couldn't read. My mouth just wouldn't form the words, my brain too saturated with pain to let anything out or in. All I could do was weep and let the words I'd been working to memorize in 2 Corinthians 4 come pouring out of my mouth, out of my heart: "We are afflicted in every way, but not crushed; perplexed, but not driven to despair; persecuted, but not forsaken; struck down, but not destroyed. . . . So we do not lose heart. Though our outer self is wasting away, our inner self is being renewed day by day. For this light momentary affliction is preparing for us an eternal weight of glory beyond all comparison, as we look not to the things that are seen but to the things that are unseen. For the things that are seen are transient, but the things that are unseen are eternal" (vv. 8–9, 16–18).

I don't know what I would've done if those words hadn't been there already, working for months in my heart to fan the flame of a growing love for the eternal, the things still to come. If eternity hadn't felt big, I think the way the world caved in would have done me in.

The feeble, distant faith in God I'd had in the past wouldn't have been enough to buoy me into an eternal perspective as I floated in a sea of grief. I think I would've turned back angry, distrustful of a distant God who took my dear friend away from parents and family and friends so early in life when the years still stretched out long and nebulous before me, the light of eternity so tiny on the horizon that it didn't do anything to change the present day.

But in the midst of the crushing storm, I saw His eyes. I saw the familiar love there.

"COME TO ME, ALL YOU WHO ARE WEARY AND BURDENED, AND I WILL GIVE YOU REST" (MATTHEW 11:28 NIV).

So we come, and He makes good on His promises. We find He's solid. Today He catches my tears. One day soon He'll wipe them away. Every single one.

As much as I long for that day when everything is set right, it's not here yet. It's still on the far side of death, and the only way to get there is by following the beckoning of a Savior who faced death for us and loves us more than we can understand. Following Him one more day. And then another. We make the choice the moment our eyes pop open in the morning. We trust He'll get us through the day before our feet ever hit the floor.

The more we do that, the more faithful we realize He is, the more we realize how much He wants us to know Him. To let Him carry us. To come out on the other side with a heart more in tune with His. And more and more, we realize we want that at any cost.

Corrie ten Boom said that one day when all of this is over, God will turn over the tapestry, unroll the canvas, and let us see the whole picture. That's going to be a beautiful day. But today is not it. Today I just have to trust Him, that as He stitches the story, He knows exactly what He's doing. *That He's working all things together for the good of those who love Him.* That He's bringing beauty from the ashes.

That He's weaving something more beautiful than I could ever imagine.

This side of heaven, I'll never know the whole picture. But even so, as I stare at the threads, the mess, I thank Him for the fact that I know He's purposeful in my life. For the things I see, and even greater, the things I can't.

When I felt God say *go*, I moved to England, and my path collided with Clare's, just after she met Jesus. Two years later, just after I moved back to the States, she passed away.

I WAS THERE IN JUST THE RIGHT WINDOW OF TIME TO HAVE HER AS A FRIEND, TO HAVE HER IMPACT MY FAITH ON A DEEP LEVEL.

God did that. In the moments of my deepest grief, when I lay facedown on the floor, forehead pressed to the carpet, tears pouring out from a bottomless well, my heart whispered the question, *Why did I have to go through this?*

But even as I've thought it, I know I wouldn't change it. No way. I praise Him that my times are in His hands, and that He put me there on purpose at just the right time, and that I got the privilege of knowing her this side of heaven. I know God better because I knew Clare. And I know God better from having the sweet privilege of grieving her death alongside her family and friends. Because of her life, I have been spurred to greater passion for Him, spurred to want to glow like she did, to love like she did. And because I was among those who had to lose her, I got to know the value of God's exquisite grace poured out in the moments when I couldn't even breathe.

His comfort is sweeter. He is sweeter. *And that's just what I can see.* One day the tapestry is going to be turned over, and we will *see it all.* We'll know why things had to happen the way they did, what God was doing when He wrote our stories the way He did. We will see how, through it all, in His unfathomable love, He's bringing glory to Himself, and He's making me holy and ready for heaven. Where I will dwell with Him forever. Where He is the ultimate prize of my life.

We'll see His redemption of the agony and discomfort and sickness roaming around this broken world. We'll see the things He shielded us from, the fate we could've had if He hadn't cared so deeply and intimately for us that He would do whatever it took to guard our souls for heaven. We will see what He did with our mess, the use He had for our dark threads, and we will worship. We'll say *it was worth it. He was worth it.* Because the story we'll see woven there will take our breath away.

HOW DOES IT CHANGE THE WAY YOU VIEW SUFFERING TO KNOW THAT IT IS PREPARING US—IN LOVE—FOR GOD'S KINGDOM?

_____

_____

_____

_____

_____

_____

_____

_____

_____

_____

_____

_____

_____

_____

_____

_____

_____

_____

ten

WE HAVE A CHOICE

Snow swirled and danced across the dry surface of the interstate, blown in intricate patterns by the passing traffic. In between the lanes, long rows of salt and snow framed the artwork happening behind the wheels of the car in front of us.

I'm not going to lie. I wasn't even driving, and I was tense on the inside. Oh, but not Abi. The brand-new Colorado resident was loving this. When the polar vortex rolled in and shook the temps down from sunny and sixty-five to subzero and snowy in a matter of hours, she went from "it's not time for Christmas yet" to wearing Santa socks to work. And in this winter traffic situation—super stressful to this southern girl—she was cruising with a cup of coffee in one hand, steering wheel in the other, looking around at the flurries like a kid experiencing the Walmart toy section for the very first time.

And I did what I do when I get wound up on the inside. Talk. Poke the introvert with a little anxiety, and words come spilling out. Words. About. Nothing.

I think I was talking about the old piano I used to have in Alabama when Abi turned to me with a grin, held up her hand, and said, "Shhhh. This song is amazing. Listen."

It was a classical piece, a cello and piano duet, and I'll admit it *was* pretty amazing. The snowflakes were swirling with the music, and as the strings went into the coda of the piece, I think I could almost see tears pooling in Abi's eyes as she sat there in her winter reverie.

"I just think there's something holy about this kind of weather," she said. "It's so beautiful. I love my commute when it's like this."

Like *this*. Fifteen miles per hour for more than an hour, the occasional slick spot, thousands of untrustworthy cars sliding around the road with her like toddlers turned loose on skates. All I wanted to do was nervously chat my way through it, like I'd do at the doctor's office. I don't know what to do with myself in a place where the tires believe it's okay to have a mind of their own. This is just the kind of weather that no one in Alabama would dare get out in for fear that they would end up stranded in their car for days on the interstate.

But in the middle of this slippery, treacherous insanity, Abi was having a moment of pure worship in her soul.

A moment of cello-accompanied, coffee-sipping worship. And she was trying to get me on board.

It was white everywhere. So much white. My landlord in England had probably meant for whoever leased the place to paint it. I'm pretty sure the white wasn't even a top coat of paint—I think it was primer, because if you pushed my black Ikea couch up against it too hard, it came away with a little layer of white dust.

I didn't care. I loved that little house. It was quirky in the way a lot of British digs are—a very old house split into several flats and updated on the inside. My flat claimed the front door, which opened into a tall entryway and the steepest staircase I think I'd ever seen up to that point. At the top of the staircase, the stairs spiraled around, and all the rooms opened into the stairs.

I was constantly falling down in that house. But I loved it.

The front overlooked a small street on which tiny cars, double-decker buses, and owners of dogs with sweaters kindly worked together to give everyone enough space to move around. The view out the back was of a beautiful historic Anglican church and cemetery. Every Sunday the bells would peal through the mist and make their way into my kitchen.

EVERY OUNCE OF ME LOVED THIS PLACE. AND THE STORY I WROTE FOR MYSELF NEVER WOULD HAVE BROUGHT ME HERE.

I would've missed so much. On that little black Ikea couch, where I read the Word and talked with God every morning, He showed me more of Himself than I had ever known before as I spent time in His Word.

It was like He came down and met with me there in southern England. And I was like a sponge, just wanting more. Several days a week I'd bundle up and walk down the street and past the park to my favorite tea shop, a super cute vintage place with scones so famously good, the lady who made them every morning wouldn't let anyone baby-sit her kids for fear they might steal the recipe from her kitchen.

I'd drop way too many sugar cubes into way too many cups of tea over hours there with my girls. In hindsight, we might've been their most valuable customers. Over all those cups of tea, those friends became my British family. And we had some seriously amazing conversations. Deep things happened.

Every Thursday night a group of guys and girls in their twenties would pile in a living room until it was bursting at the seams to study the Bible and pray together. The group grew and grew, and so did we. So did the light in our eyes.

It would take pages and pages to write down everything I saw God do in my life and in the lives of the people I met during those two years in England. It would also take a lot of pages to write down how much fun it was.

GOD'S HAND WAS ON THAT SEASON IN A WAY I'D NEVER EXPERIENCED BEFORE.

I felt like Peter when he stood on the mountaintop with Jesus and suddenly Jesus shone bright as a light, and Moses and Elijah showed up too. "Lord, it's good that we're here. Let me make a tent for all of us so we can just stay."

God had brought me here, and He was bright and close, so I wanted to do the same thing Peter did. Stay. It was then that I finally hung pictures on those white walls, something it had taken me a year and a half to get around to doing. Barely two weeks after I'd hammered in the nails, I found out I was going to have to leave.

I took a couple of deep breaths before I put Abi's car in reverse and rolled back a few inches, snow crunching under the tires. She'd given the Alabama girl a short tutorial in proper snow driving and then tossed me the keys with a grin and a parting remark. "Remember, you break it, you buy it."

Oh gosh. I really didn't want to have to buy it.

Why is anyone in their right mind out here? Why am I? Go home, people. Take a leaf out of Alabama's book and stay home.

But if that guy in the snow-covered Accord from Florida can do it, so can I. Right? *God, please help me. I really don't want to have to replace a midsize SUV.* As I sat there with my foot on the brake, snowflakes swirled around each other and landed on the windshield. I stared at them, my eyes tracing their tiny outlines. *Crazy.*

Crazy that something so beautiful could cause so much anxiety. Crazy that something that looks so good from above could, from the angle of the ground, look like it wants to kill me. Crazy that life's a lot like that too. God and I naturally view things pretty differently. And my natural perspective is a lot closer to the ground.

I lay there on the floor, right in the center, equidistant from all four white, white walls, and I tried my best to process the news. The rules had changed a bit over the past two years, and the kind of residency visa I had couldn't be renewed.

I'm not going to lie. I was pretty devastated. As the reality soaked in, I realized something else. Rewind again to that park bench where I said good-bye to that guy, the friendship that had to end because God had led me to move to England . . . and then rewind just a few months further back. I was at a table with the man who was working up the contract details for my job in England, and he asked me what seemed like an insignificant question.

"Do you want to commit to two years or three?"

I thought for a minute. "If I sign up for two, I can extend it to stay longer, right?"

"Yes."

"So in reality, it doesn't really matter which I choose now. I can stay either way."

"Yes."

That budding relationship flashed in my mind. *God, I don't know what is going to happen with that. Only You do. It's seemed like You've been leading us both to explore this intentionally, but it's still so new, and it's very possible it won't work out. But if things do keep progressing, more than two years would be a really long time to be gone.*

"I'll sign up for two. But I'll most likely stay longer."

"Great."

It seemed so trivial at the time, but now I realized . . . it was going to change everything. If I'd signed up for a longer contract, I would've had a different kind of visa. And I could've stayed. Lying there, I took it all in, and I took a deep breath.

God, I'm so sad. I'm so sad to see this era drawing to a close. This really has been a mountaintop experience, and I would've loved for it to last a lifetime. I couldn't believe I was going to have to say good-bye when I felt like I had just settled in. Where would I go? What would I do instead? The thoughts rushed in like snowflakes on the interstate, winding me into a tight panic like that Denver commute, squeezing tears from my eyes. *God, I can't see anything up ahead right now.*

But I thought back a few weeks to a different day, a different snow. I was on a trip for work, and I was sitting in my hotel room, book in hand, watching the flakes fall outside the window. The book was written by a girl named Katie Davis who was so moved by the orphans she met on a visit to Uganda that she moved there to take care of them . . . when she was eighteen. She adopted thirteen of them, and she's doing her best to take care of all the rest who live anywhere near her.

Amazing. God had done so much for her, she felt the least she could do was to be His vessel to love the ones who didn't yet know His love. *What a story He was writing through her. For her. For those little girls. For His glory.*

My heart welled up in response to her story, to the simple and poignant way she described what she had felt, the way God filled her heart to overflowing with love for Uganda's children. I was barely through the book's introduction when I found myself on my knees, saying it all over again like I had that day in front of the cross.

"GOD, IT'S ALL STILL YOURS. YOU CAN HAVE IT ALL. YOU CAN MOVE ME WHEREVER YOU WANT, ANYTIME."

That day three weeks later, lying on the floor in my flat in England, even though I was sad, I knew that's exactly what God was doing. He was moving me where He wanted. It wasn't a mistake that I'd made that decision three years ago. I'd been seeking Him with my whole life that day when I made that "little" contract choice, not just seeking Him in that one decision. And I'd been seeking Him that day that Katie Davis's book made me hit my knees on the hotel room floor.

GOD HAD MY LIFE, MY DREAMS, MY PLANS. I'D GIVEN THEM TO HIM. WHEN WE LIVE LIKE THAT, WE TRUST THAT HE WORKS IN ALL OUR DECISIONS, BIG AND SMALL.

We don't have to agonize over the small stuff—or the big stuff, for that matter. We pray. We live and move and have our being in Him. We can trust Him to know the big picture, even when it doesn't make sense, even when we don't realize the "small" decisions we make are actually big ones.

Like with that almost-relationship. I may not know all the reasons it happened. But I do know this: God used it to grow me. He used it to move me. He knew He would want to take me out of England at exactly that time. And when I told Him everything was His, that's exactly what He did. It was the next thread in the story He was weaving, and in including it, He answered my prayers. *More of You, God. Whatever that means.*

On the day that "whatever" meant leaving England, I was wiping away tears when Bex handed the thick, red scarf to me. We were standing just outside the security line in London's Heathrow Airport in the middle of the afternoon on a weekday. I'd said good-bye to most of my friends the night before over curry at a local Indian restaurant. We'd tried to make the evening as normal as possible. We'd had a great time.

We'd dawdled in the parking lot, goofing off and saying good-bye, none of us wanting to leave. It was the last time I'd see them for a while. It was the last time I'd see Clare on earth, though I didn't know it. The next day my friend Harriet had driven me and all my bags to the airport in a car packed to the gills, and Bex had met me there on the train and walked me to the point where she couldn't go any farther. She'd sent me off with a hug and that warm, red scarf.

"If it snows in Alabama this winter, I'll be ready now," I said, laughing through tears.

"It will remind you of home," she said.

Perfect.

As I walked away and headed off to my gate, I knew that right that moment I was walking through a different kind of snow, the kind that keeps you from seeing very far in front of you, the kind that dusts everything in uniform mystery.

I had no idea what I was heading into.

ADULTHOOD WAS TAKING ANOTHER UNEXPECTED TURN, AND IT WAS TOTALLY OUT OF MY CONTROL, TOTALLY OUT OF MY COMFORT ZONE.

I had no idea what was coming, or how long it would last. But what Abi said about the Colorado snow applied here too. *There's something holy about it.*

I thought that a few months into her first Colorado winter, Abi might take back the claim she'd made that day in the car to love all things snowy. I was wrong. I asked her about it again, asked her what she loved about it so much, and excitement came bubbling out of her in flowery words like some kind of love poem.

She said one thing that made it feel so holy was that it was the catalyst for new life, moisture coming down to the dead, dry ground in "sparkling glory."

"It's like the whole earth stops and holy glittering redemption blankets the barrenness," she said. "I just feel God's presence in it, like a sunset or a mountain."

God's presence in it. Maybe that's it. Maybe that's exactly why it's holy. Maybe it's because when it comes, if we let our anxiety go, we *feel His presence in it*, and in the moment when heaven meets earth, we see God again. And maybe at that moment life is renewed again.

It happened to Peter that way. Peter might've been a little hasty in wanting to put up a tent for Jesus, Moses, and Elijah up on that mountain, but one thing's for sure:

CALM OR STORM, IF HE SAW JESUS' DIVINE PRESENCE ANYWHERE NEAR HIM, HE JUST KNEW HE WANTED MORE OF IT.

It was wind, not snow, that worked Peter and the other disciples into a panic one night on a boat ride to the other side of the sea. The waves and the wind were beating against the boat like crazy. And in the middle of all that, Jesus came walking toward them. On the water. They thought He was a ghost.

"But immediately Jesus spoke to them, saying, 'Take heart; it is I. Do not be afraid'" (Matthew 14:27). I don't know if the rest of them stopped freaking out, or if they still had their fingernails dug into their seats like I did in Abi's SUV, but Peter let go of the panic. No—he did better than that.

"Lord, if it is you, command me to come to you on the water" (v. 28). And Jesus said, "Come" (v. 29). And Peter did.

Peter looked up in the storm, saw Jesus there, and stepped out of the boat to go to Him. And as long as he kept his eyes on Jesus, he *walked on the water* in the middle of that storm. It's when he looked down that he sunk. *And we are the same way.*

That truth is something I might as well seal in my heart now, because it will never change: from mountaintop to stormy sea, big green hill in England to Mississippi River levee, God never meant for me to stake a claim here on earth, on what's under my feet. He meant for me to keep my eyes on Him and *follow*, even if that looked different from other people, even if that looked a little crazy. Even if it hurt.

HE WANTS US TO WALK WITH HIM.

And He is what we want.

I was ready to pitch tents in England because I felt His presence there. But when I realized He was in the storm, when I realized He was moving me on again, His presence became the reason I was okay with walking away.

He stands out there in the storm, in everything I can't see. But I hear His voice, and He calls to me, "Come." Out of desire for Him—nothing else—I say my good-byes, and I step out into the storm, into the waters I've never walked on before.

Most of us don't like the fact that our adulthood is a little bit snow-covered and unclear. I'll admit I've really never been a fan of snow. I'm still learning to pry my fingernails out of the sides of the passenger seat. But in our unexpected twists and turns, He beckons us, "Come. I'm here. And it will be okay."

So you see it comes down to one thing. Every day I have a choice. I can focus on how life doesn't look like I wanted it to, how it's moving at a crawl, the way the road's too slippery, the way the outlook on the ground is gross or frustrating or exhausting for miles and miles. I can worry if something much worse is going to happen if I walk on into what's ahead of me.

Or I can choose a song. I can choose to sip my coffee

slowly and keep my eyes on the goodness tumbling down from the sky, choose to keep my heart in a place of total, unwavering praise.

BECAUSE HE'S THERE IN MY SNOWSTORM.

He's there to be seen and enjoyed and reveled in and worshipped. He's there to blanket my hurt in a fresh layer of His pure white love. It falls and it falls. And it just keeps coming. "[Your mercies] are new every morning; great is your faithfulness" (Lamentations 3:23).

There *is* something holy about the way the most treacherous times are the most beautiful, the darkest times the most full of God's complete covering of love. There's a lot of wonder in the way He shows us Himself in the moments when we don't think we can go another step, when in anxiety we finally tilt our chin up to look at Him. To look at heaven.

His love falls on us visibly. Softly. Like a dance. Like a comforter. It's a reality that prompts childlike wonder, the wonder of Christmas and fireplaces and gifts and sparkling snowflakes falling from the sky and hitting your tongue. It's pieces of heaven coming down that pile in our hearts and remind us of who our Father is.

It's as good as it gets. And it often comes in the middle of as hard as it gets. I'm not saying we love pain. Do we sing when there's sunshine? Sure. But we live in a broken world, a world where rough roads are inevitable. And we have a God kind enough to rig it so the hardest moments allow us the chance to see Him the best—the fullest—to experience His love most deeply. That means everything from the sun to the snow is ultimately *good*. Good things here and even better things later *for those who love Him.*

NO MATTER WHAT, WE WIN.

So I have a choice. I can choose to worry. Or I can choose to keep living my life, keep chasing after a God who's never failed me yet, who's only become deeper, richer, fuller with every time, every snowflake, every mile. I think I'll take that one. Today. And again tomorrow. With that choice, I'll take another step into His story.

HOW DOES IT CHANGE YOUR PERSPECTIVE TO SAY AGAIN TO GOD TODAY, "EVERYTHING I HAVE IS YOURS. EVERY PIECE OF MY LIFE, I TRUST YOU WITH IT." _____

_____

_____

_____

_____

eleven

THE NEW NORMAL

My shoes thudded on the blacktop as the rosy Alabama sunset settled across the rooftops. The houses sat back from the road all quiet and lazy, and fireflies poked specks of light into the shadows that were starting to pool in the yards.

Everything was golden. Rush-hour traffic had long made it home for dinner, and any young children still up at this point were probably on their second or third round of begging for a later bedtime. The cicadas were the only things other than my shoes generating noise, and I don't think either of us minded the other being there.

Summer was officially open for business, and I was happy to be its first customer. I'd been pounding the pavement of this route for what seemed like ages before the season finally came that washed it with sun. I knew the road's dips and cracks without being able to see them, and for months I'd stuck to the same freezing, pitch-black path each day after work, eyes straight ahead, bouncing from the small glow of one streetlight to the next. That kind of run wasn't my favorite, but it got the job done.

In the summer, though, everything was different. It was *pure joy*. The exercise itself wasn't necessarily better in the summer—in fact, I sweated a lot harder, took a lot longer, went a lot slower. But my eyes were wide open, the details pouring in at a rate I couldn't keep up with. A brilliant deluge pumped my heart full of life—and just kept pumping.

That was the power of summer.

IMAGINE WHEN THE POWER OF GOD GETS INJECTED INTO OUR "NORMAL."

The reality of His universe-shattering affection puts us on sensory overload. It won't fit inside the skin of my everyday life. It won't fit inside me or inside my world. My friend Clare put it this way: *The heart you've got just isn't big enough to hold all of God's love for you. It bursts the heart you have. So you're going to need a new heart—a bigger one.*

You'll need a bigger life too. But not bigger in the sense that it's more serious or more adventurous or more visible. At least not necessarily. It's just that once you experience

God's love, you'll need a life with new skin on it, skin that can wrap around heart-bursting joy and live to tell about it. Skin that feels the tingling sensation in the air that *God is everywhere, and so is His love, and there's nothing bigger to be had.*

When that sinks in, instead of feeling that yawning chasm behind you, you have the feeling of something pulling you upward, pushing you on. It gives life momentum. But it does something else too. It pops a new set of eyes in your head. You can't help but see the pockets of profound darkness around you, or the people who still live in it. You want desperately for them to see what you see, to feel what you feel. To experience freedom.

Those people, they press on your heart. And they keep your eyes open as you lie in bed at night, with a whole different set of questions than the ones that used to roll around in your head—questions like these: *What will it take for them to see too? With the life I've been given, how can I best help that happen?*

When we'd first arrived in their little huddle of tents in the Himalayas, they spotted our foreign faces, and you could almost see their pupils turn into dollar signs. Not that I blame them—there was only one plausible reason we'd traveled all the way out there: to rent their horses and head off into the mountains. Never mind that it was pouring rain.

They didn't know how to ask us in English, but they could pantomime it for us, and if that wasn't enough, by the end of the conversation, I had the nose of a conveniently placed (albeit very wet) horse poking me in the back.

My friend Cierra could speak the regional language, and she told them, "We don't want to ride a horse. We want to sit in your tent with you and have tea and talk."

"Really?"

"Yes."

"No horse?"

"No."

Well then. Come on.

The four of us and eight of them piled into a small but very warm tent, cramming as close to the stove in the center as we could. A lady with rosy cheeks ladled prepared yak milk tea from a pot on the stove into bowls and pushed them into our hands.

Within seconds they were joking and laughing with us, and we were giving the main horseman language lessons. Or at least one phrase—"Ride a horse." It had obvious marketing benefits. But then Cierra had something else for them.

In their language, she asked them if they'd ever heard of the Most High God. They laughed. They were sharing their tent with an idol, and around their tents, strings of brightly colored prayer flags were flapping in the rainy breeze, blessing the surrounding countryside in the name of another god. Darkness enveloped them.

She told them about Him anyway. The whole tent heard, some truly listening. Afterward, all four of us sang them a song in English, and they scrambled for their smartphones. Then Cierra and another friend, Becky, sang a song about Him for them in their language, and they recorded it.

My God, I worship You.

My heart loves You deeply.

At Your throne, I think of Your grace.

My heart praises and worships.

My God, I want to worship You.

I watched our hosts' faces, all of them caught up in the way the foreigners sang so passionately about a God they had never heard of. Maybe, just maybe, they'll listen to the song the crazy white girls sang again sometime, and they'll think about the story they heard. Who knows what happens to things when they end up in the belly of a smartphone. But there was one thing I did know as I sat there. Over yak milk tea, God wrecked my heart all over again for the people of the world who don't know the peace of a Savior and Friend who gives us a hope and a future. The darkness and its victims now had faces in my mind, in my heart. And that was never going to go away.

I sat there in the quiet holding a cup of black tea made the British way, with a little spot of milk poured in. The thick blackness of predawn Alabama cradled the house as I chugged caffeine and rubbed the grit from my eyes.

So much darkness. I can't handle it. It was 4:50 a.m. I'm a morning person, but this felt like the middle of the night. *Here we go, God. Here's the new normal.*

That was my first day at a new job, a job forty-five minutes away from the house where I was living in the suburbs, a job that was going to make me get up crazy early in order to have time with Jesus in the mornings. *This isn't going to be easy.* That thought was loud as the steam rose from my cup, silence blanketing the house.

At my other job, I'd grown used to having plenty of time in the mornings to lay out my day before God, trying to set my heart to let Him order the minutes as He chose, trying to see in His Word that my life is not my own. That process had changed me. But I knew my own weakness. I remembered those years when I'd picked myself and my own desires, and I was afraid that with this new schedule, slowly I'd slip into a routine of picking myself every time again. Exhaustion would win out. Selfishness would win out. The feeling that life was business as usual would win out, and I wouldn't expect divine plot twists to happen in my normal day.

With less and less time spent with God, eternity and the desire for it would lose their golden glow and melt down into just one earthly desire, back to the one thing I'd wanted for myself—I'd find myself wishing there was someone there to sit on the couch with me when I got home at night.

No, my heart whispered. *I don't want to feel that way again.* I felt God whisper back, *It doesn't have to be that way.*

I squeezed my eyes shut, grasping at those words, wanting to feel their truth all the way to the depths of my heart.

I WANTED THEM TO PLANT THEMSELVES THERE AND GROW INTO A NEW KIND OF NORMAL.

God, please let this year and every one after that be marked with You, marked with a different way to live. Please let me see my life, my time, and my choices the way You see them. Through Your eyes. And please help me remember that even the most normal day is full of Your story.

It was a pretty normal day this past fall when I met Naomi at a coffeehouse in Denver. She'd asked me about a necklace I was wearing—one that had my name written in another language—and she pulled back her sleeve to show me a tattoo on her wrist that looked a little bit like it. It wasn't the same language, but they were in the same family.

"What's it say?"

"It says, 'Love through His eyes.'"

I grinned. "I'm going to need to hear the story behind that one."

My new friend was a barista at my temporary office, and I had a feeling it might be a while before I got to hear her tattoo story. I also had a feeling it was going to be worth the wait. I was right.

I picked up my tea, got out of the massive line, and settled in to work in one of the coffeehouse's big leather chairs. The mountains poked up in the distance outside the window. I popped in a pair of earbuds, preparing to use Pandora to tune out Denver's caffeine-deprived masses.

I had a lot of work to do that day, and apparently a lot of other people did too. Or at least they had a lot of coffee to drink.

I'd long since made it to the bottom of my cup of tea before she pulled up a chair and sat down beside me. The line had finally dwindled away, and the place had hit that comfortable hum that coffeehouses do when everyone's happily caffeinated, earbuds in, working on whatever it is we're all working on.

I pulled out my earbuds. "Okay, I'm ready." I was excited.

Naomi began to tell me the story of her tattoo. She said

there was a certain group of people on the other side of the world that she'd never been too sure about, one that made her a little more nervous than any of the others. "I'd been playing a game one night with some friends, and one of the questions was, 'If you had to get rid of one country, which one would you choose?'" She knew immediately which one she'd pick. She hadn't realized how strong her feelings were about it until that game.

But funny enough, God used another game to begin to turn it all around. She was playing a game online one day when she found herself playing against someone from that particular country. They struck up a conversation in the game's chat window. The conversation kept going for quite a while, and her son walked into the room and asked her whom she was talking to. She said it was a new friend in that country.

Her son said, "Mom, did you know God loves them as much as He loves you?"

That was all it took.

HER ANIMOSITY BEGAN TO MELT INTO LOVE, THE LOVE THAT CHRIST HAD FOR THOSE PEOPLE.

Love through His eyes.
"At that moment I was allowed to see others through the

eyes of God. Everything was immediately filtered through love. I knew I would never be the same." She paused. "You're a believer, right?"

I smiled. "Right."

"I knew it. I could see the light in your eyes."

God, I sure do hope that's true.

But one thing was for sure—I had actually had that thought about *her*, from the minute I'd first ended up in her line at the cash register. And I know I'm not the only one. Dozens of people come by her register every day. People from that country she loves also find their way into her line sometimes, and when they do, the light shines brightly. She met two women the other day who came in for coffee, and it was instant friendship.

"We got to go to their family's restaurant later, and they greeted us like family. It was so great."

As I listened to her story, I felt God whisper it again: *My story is a really, really big one. Really big, yet really personal. And nothing about it—not even the "normal"—is mundane.*

It was a normal American birthday. Maybe just a little extra crazy. The pizza dough was ripping in midair, balloons were rolling around underfoot, and laughter filled the kitchen. Underneath the tinsel Happy Birthday crown that was tucked over Mariam's headscarf, her dark eyes were taking it all in.

In the midst of the fray, Elizabeth grabbed her by the shoulder and wrote a ridiculous song on the spot. "It's your birthday! And there's pizza with holes. And we love you."

Both laughed, and Elizabeth walked away to the table full of food, not even hearing the birthday girl's whispered response: "Thank you."

It had been almost a year since our paths first crossed hers. She didn't know a lot of words in our language. She couldn't drive. And she didn't really know what to do here in our southern city with no sidewalks and no bilinguals, and no friends or family within a 6,000-mile radius. We felt for her.

So my friend Callie and I started hanging out with her on Wednesday nights at her apartment. Over really, really strong coffee, she started teaching us her language. I was bad at it. Really, really bad. But she looked past that, thankfully. We became friends, muddling our way through with very little common language.

We circled around the same topics. We talked about her family. We talked about how hot Alabama's summers are. And we always ended up on a particular favorite subject of hers—her upstairs neighbor, Ashley.

Ashley was a music student at a local college, and she stopped in to see our friend often. She took her to the store. She brought her fresh flowers. She helped her with paperwork and figuring out how to find things.

"Ashley is goodness to me. She is goodness," Mariam would say, putting her hand up to her heart.

Who is this Ashley? I thought.

She has to be a believer, because what she's doing sure does look a whole lot like Jesus.

Turns out she was. We found Ashley a few weeks later by way of a chance meeting in the parking lot, and came to find out she'd been praying for God to bring people from other cultures into her life to stretch her, to let her have a place to pour Christ's love on thirsty ground right in her own city.

Then Mariam moved into her building, and Ashley started praying for more. She started praying for more believers to come into our friend's life to show her what loving community looks like.

"You guys are the answer to that prayer," she told us.

I was stunned. It felt a lot more like Ashley was the answer to mine. When I'd been overseas, it was like something in me had broken. Just like when I first caught a real glimpse of God and knew I never wanted to view life the same way again, I'd caught a glimpse of His heart for the world, for the hurting, and I never wanted to go back to living life blind.

People like those Himalayan horsemen had taught me something. I wanted to see the people around me, no matter where I was—especially the ones who found themselves as strangers, fatherless, and without families. And hopeless. I wanted to seek them out. I wanted to live like my time wasn't my own. I just had no idea how to do that in normal American life. Enter Ashley.

She was getting it done. She was praying for God to bring those people into her midst. She was seeking them out. She was pouring her time into them in intentional, practical, sacrificial ways. I began to try to follow the example she was modeling.

It wasn't long before Callie and I were going on some of the most terrifying practice drives of our life, helping our friend paint her living room, and getting late-night texts asking for help with job applications. It was definitely stretching. But it was the beginning of a really good new normal.

Ann Voskamp says that our time is precious, like diamonds. It's short, friends. It's short. Even if you were to live a full ninety years. If a .05 carat diamond were used to represent each week of those 90 years, they'd barely fill up a tablespoon. *That's a really, really small amount of very precious time.* And we aren't even guaranteed that much.

We don't have time to settle. We don't have minutes to just throw away.

It would be a sad way of spending our spoonfuls, she says, to waste each diamond wishing we had a better one, thinking that this one wasn't good enough. Thinking that God wasn't good enough. Thinking everything would be better if we had houses, or husbands, or children, or someone else's story.

In the weeks and months before I fell at the foot of that cross and gave God my little spoonful of diamonds, I'd been listening to my pastor speak every week about how we've been given a gift—a few diamonds, and a whole lot of hope in God. As he shook me awake with his words, he reminded me that there are a whole lot of people who don't even know that hope exists. *My whole life, my whole eternity hinges on it . . . and they don't even know it exists.*

I'd been just doing my thing as those people watched their diamonds play out, and they slipped into a Christless eternity. *Where suffering never, ever goes away.* I couldn't shake the feeling that there was no way the version of normal I'd been living was okay in light of that.

When I live the kind of normal where I work, do my thing, and sit on the couch at night just wishing someone else was there with me, I let my own desires become the big deal. And I get lulled into forgetting that the whole world is a lot bigger than my little house. I forget that my whole world should be oriented around a God who offers everything *and around the billions of people who have yet to know Him.*

Like the people in that country that Naomi loves. Like those horsemen and their families in the foothills of the Himalaya. Like the Ryans of the world, just waiting for a foster parent like Heather to take them in, love them like Jesus, and tell them He can change their whole lives.

Because the truth is that He's writing my story into something amazing, something better than I could've come up with on my own.

HIS STORY IS A LOT BIGGER THAN JUST ME.

Yes, He cares about the intimate details of my life because He loves me. Because He cares for me enough to refine me and make me holy for heaven. The pages of my story scream that those things are true. I've seen them.

But His love is big, and it stretches to the other side of the world to reach into the hearts of Himalayan horsemen. He loves them enough to send Cierra and Becky and a whole troupe of other people to share the hope sitting in their hearts. He loves orphans in Uganda enough to prick the heart of a Tennessee homecoming queen named Katie Davis and draw her to be their mom. Because those girls, their stories were never about just them. And my story has never been about just me.

Go into all the world and tell everyone about the hope that you have. Show them how to follow Me. Show them how I'm Life itself. What God says He sees as true religion is this: to care for the widows, the orphans, the people in distress. And that's how people know we belong to Him—*by our love.* It's not just about doing something. It's not just about feeling something. It's both. It has to be both.

Our whole life is about knowing Him and making Him known. That's what we're here for. That's *all* we're here for. Because no matter where we are, Alabama or Africa, it's always all on the table, not just in theory, but in actuality. Even the most normal day was never meant to be about me.

Back in Alabama, back in the 8-to-5 world where things have the tendency to slip into autopilot, I found myself lying there in the dark one night, eyes wide open, thoughts buzzing in my head. My mind replayed a conversation from earlier in the day.

"Any idea when it's going to happen?"

"Not really. He's still got to get the ring made."

"Do you know what the diamond's going to look like?"

"I'm not totally sure what he's planning to do with it, but I'm pretty sure the band will be yellow gold."

I'd asked my friend, who was in a relationship headed toward marriage, if she was okay with that plan.

"Yeah, I like gold. I don't have much gold jewelry, but I guess this will make me become more of a gold girl."

As I lay there with the words circling around in my head, it was like my heart reached down into my proverbial pocket, felt to see if the "gold" was still there, jingled it around a little bit, and said, *Yep. I may not hear those desires loudly anymore, but they haven't left completely. I'm definitely still a girl.*

In a matter of weeks, three of my close friends had all been hit out of the blue with the affection of three very godly men, and each seemed to fit them perfectly. Each served and loved them like Christ in a way I hadn't seen happen much among my peers. It was really beautiful. It made me smile to watch the way all three of those ladies— each of them fiercely independent, each of them walking firmly in their singleness in Christ—just couldn't help it.

They saw Jesus in these guys' eyes, and they fell despite themselves. I was genuinely happy for each of them. But as I lay there in bed that night, a thought crept into my mind for the first time in a long time. And I went ahead and said it to God, because I knew He already saw it in my heart. *God, I'm very much content with the story You've written for me. I wouldn't trade anything You've done so far for a different story, or for anyone else's. I wouldn't trade England. I wouldn't trade being exactly where You've put me and getting to visit my friends on the other side of the world and seeing the faces of those people who still need to know Your hope, getting to share Your love with the people in my path.*

But I thought about my three friends and the guys pursuing them, and I smiled to myself. *I'll admit, though, if You wanted to bring a guy like that along, I wouldn't complain.* Even as I said it, I felt myself weighing the desire in my hand. It was there. But it wasn't heavy anymore. In fact, it felt pretty light. *Praise God for that.*

The other day a single friend asked me, "When you get to the point where Jesus is enough, is it that your battle with being single is hard, hard, hard"—she moved her hand across the air like she was drawing a straight line on a graph—"then Jesus is enough," she said, drawing a peak that then sloped back down to the first line, "then hard, hard, hard?"

"Or," she asked, "do you get to a point where Jesus is just enough, period?"

All I can say is that for me there was a definitive point where it changed, and that point was at the foot of that cross propped in the corner of that prayer room. When I laid everything down that day, when I jumped, when He changed my desires from the inside out, those dreams faded to the point that they almost had no voice at all. Part of that process was the way He filled up my heart with desires that led me back to Him and to His Word, and that changed the way I felt about the old desires.

But another part of that reality was when that freedom fleshed itself out in obedience, my hands and feet were busy, and I didn't have time to think I was missing something.

I WAS BEING FILLED UP BY HIS LOVE THROUGH HIS WORD.

I was being filled up by the joy I got from pouring out that love on others, whether by doing a friend's dishes or talking through a problem over tea or sharing the gospel with someone who had never heard that beautiful story before.

There wasn't a lot of room for much else anymore, and that was a very, very good thing. It had changed my whole life, my whole outlook on life. It had created an amazing new normal, and I didn't want any of His fullness to leak out of my heart. I didn't want there to be room for anything else. I wanted more moments where I get to seek out those who need hope and show them where it's found. I wanted more moments where I see His deliberate hand in carving sin out of my life, more moments where I get to stay up late talking with a friend who needs someone to talk to. Because those moments are precious. And they're not about me.

But the joy that comes from getting to be a part of them is unfathomable. A gift from an unfathomable God.

I've been thinking about this—this choosing to let go of our dreams thing in relation to our view of who God is to us, Amy B wrote me the other day. She said she'd been thinking about how it makes a difference knowing the unfathomable, edgeless God—because *that* kind of God is the only One trustworthy enough for us to throw our lives into His arms with abandon. *I've been studying Romans 9, and this verse had new meaning to me because of that thought: "But who are you, O man, to answer back to God? Will what is molded say to its molder, 'Why have you made me like this?'" (v. 20). I think it is so true of me, that my questions of God change the more I know who He is and how He sees me,* Amy wrote. *I mean, who am I to tell God what is best for myself and ask why my life isn't something "better"? It's ignorance, and, really, pride. After seeing who He is, it's then that I have to choose to humble myself.*

Humbling ourselves *makes sense.*

BECAUSE WHEN I HOLD MY EMPTY HANDS UP IN OBEDIENCE TO THE STORY HIS PEN IS DRAWING, THAT'S WHEN JOY COMES.

It's a joy that no earthly thing could ever bring. And that night as I lay in bed replaying that engagement ring conversation, my heart whispered a prayer, a prayer for more of that joy.

I don't know where the road between here and when I see Your face is going to lead, but I want You to determine the steps, for my good and for Your glory. You know what I don't know, and You see what I don't see. It's the story You've written that is playing itself out. It's bigger than I can imagine. It's good. And it's all I want.

IN WHAT WAYS MIGHT YOUR PERSPECTIVE, BEHAVIOR, AND WORDS CHANGE IF GOD GAVE YOU A "NEW PAIR OF EYES"?

twelve

FOLLOWING THE THREAD
OF THE VERY BEST STORY

I already knew what she was going to say before I even asked the question. It was really just a formality. No matter how ridiculous, if it'll make a good story, Elizabeth is always up for it. Always. That's how we've ended up places like the deck of Codzilla (Google it), a mildly terrifying amateur shrine to Elvis with a working electric chair (symbolizing "Jailhouse Rock," of course), and the midnight release party for the fourth book in the Twilight series. As full-grown adults.

To my shame, I'm the one who proposed all of those ideas, each of which was a train wreck. But Elizabeth never stopped saying yes. And that list is just the tip of the iceberg. So there wasn't really any question about where she was going to pick to have lunch that day. I'd driven three days to get to Colorado and arrived just in time to meet her plane from Alabama. We didn't plan it; it just happened that way. I was going to visit Abi for a little while, and Elizabeth was going there for a work conference.

I tried hard not to be jealous about the fact that she'd just covered a three days' drive in two hours on a plane. That was barely long enough to get in a thorough perusal of *SkyMall* magazine. And it definitely wasn't long enough for me to do any thorough research on somewhere fun to eat lunch on her one free day in the Mile High City. I didn't know anything about Denver, so my only ammo was what the Internet could tell me while I sat in the airport's cell phone waiting lot.

"I came up with a few options," I told her as she got in the car. One was a hipster gourmet hamburger joint. Another was a little café downtown that served coffee and lunch. She was okay with either. "But there's also this Mexican place . . ." I trailed off. I'd been tipped off to its existence from my friend Jana, who used to live in Colorado before she moved to England.

"IT'S THE KIND OF PLACE YOU GO FOR THE EXPERIENCE."

"Because the food isn't all that special," Jana had told me. "But you should really go. We used to go there all the time. Locals will know exactly which restaurant you're talking about, but they'll all probably wonder why you want to go there, because it's kind of ridiculous. They have a gorilla."

Weird. Okay.

So I'd pictured your normal Mexican restaurant with a gorilla statue. Or someone in a gorilla suit playing in the mariachi band. I Googled it from the cell phone waiting lot, and boy, was I wrong. This place was so much more. Billing itself as the greatest show in the city and as having mouth-watering food, it advertised a 30-foot waterfall and daring cliff divers. The show schedule said it had dive shows, gunfights, gorillas, and pirates.

"Done," Elizabeth said.

That's what I figured.

"I don't know why you even told me about the other places."

I laughed. "I have no idea what this is going to be," I said. But with marketing like that and a personal recommendation, it couldn't be too bad, right?

We were barely in the door when I knew Jana had done us wrong. Elizabeth said she knew it was all going south when we ordered our food at a cash register and then pushed our cafeteria trays down a long, long silver bar and waited for our "mouth-watering Mexican food" to come out of a hole in the wall.

When it did, we weren't sure we wanted it. It was

smothered in something that Elizabeth called "the color of plague," the whole plate a homogenous glob of fluorescent orange cheese-like substance.

"It looks like they put it under a hot light in 1982 and didn't think about it again until we placed our order," she said.

She was right. I thought, *Well, at least there's gonna be divers. Surely that will make any subpar enchilada tolerable, right?* Two bites in, and we both knew there was no way we were ever going to get the food down. So we stopped trying. We watched a girl perform a few high dives into a pool near our table, a pretty bizarre experience altogether. *Where does a Mexican restaurant go to recruit stunt divers?*

We saw a guy in a gorilla suit chase a few people around the restaurant. Within the hour, we were at that hipster burger joint. And within an hour after that, we were both not feeling so great.

"Welcome to Denver," I said with a laugh. I wondered if Elizabeth wished we could go back to the airport and make that choice over again.

The suitcases were sitting around me again, the British airline's three-bag allowance crammed full of the hand-picked most important things I owned. Like pillows. I never did figure out where to buy good ones in England.

Enough time had passed that I could apply for a visa again, so I was giving it another go. It was serious déjà vu as I packed everything up in Birmingham, said good-byes, and prepared to leave. And then something happened. The visa fell through again. I could tell you all the ins and outs of how that came to be and what it felt like, but I'm betting even without the details you can guess how that news went down—like a plague-colored enchilada.

Man. I can't believe this.

I DID THE ONLY THING I KNEW TO DO—I STARTED ASKING ABOUT THE BACKUP PLAN.

They told me there was another place I could go hang out for a little while until it was all worked out.

"Where?" I asked.

Where else . . . but the country that's the homeland of my friend Mariam, the one whose birthday we'd celebrated, the friend who'd been trying hard to teach me her language. I wished some of that language had stuck. Very little did, and now I was wishing I'd tried a lot harder.

But it was clear when that plan was tossed out to me that it had come from Someone higher, Someone who had a larger story going on than I knew about when I first went over to Mariam's house for the strongest coffee of my life.

I WAS BEING OFFERED A PLOT TWIST.

I knew it was risky, like a Mexican restaurant with a high dive. There was a chance this might not go well. But I took it.

"Grace. I owe you a *major* apology."

Texts that say things like that always make me a little nervous. While those three little dots are sitting there at the bottom of the screen, I'm running through all the things that the sender could be about to tell me, the things that could've possibly gone wrong.

"I'm at that restaurant. Apparently, it's a whole different experience when you come here as a kid. The food is *terrible*. I had no memory of it being *this* bad."

Jana. Oh, Jana.

"I think I owe you two dinner."

I'm not going to lie—it makes me feel a little better that she got to see for herself and that she didn't still think it was decent food. I think Elizabeth and I would both take her up on that dinner. But in the end, I don't think either of us would choose differently if given a do-over. We've had a lot of good but very forgettable burgers in our lifetime, but I think I can speak for both of us when I say neither of us have ever had a slightly awkward stunt-diving show take place next to our lunch conversation.

We'll never forget that place. These are the stories that are told when we sit around the dinner table with friends. We tell the story of that plague-colored cheese and the way nobody clapped when that girl just kept diving over and over. We tell a whole arsenal of stories like it from our past.

We tell the story about how our friend Christian screamed louder than any little kid on Codzilla when the water started coming over the side of the boat. We tell the story of that guy who'd framed a Kleenex he thought Elvis might've had in his pocket once, and how we weren't sure we were going to get out of his memorabilia-filled house without Emily agreeing to marry him. And we laughed really hard. That's why we'll always pick the weird Mexican restaurants of the world, even though they are a risk.

You go where the best story is.

I hate to compare any real-life decision to the choice to go to a Mexican restaurant with a high dive. I don't really want to draw many parallels there. I honestly hope I never see "cheese" like that again. But there's one thing about our decision to go there that day that stands out to me. Despite the things that we had reservations about, despite the fact that we could've chosen the standard, normal option, we knew we had to choose "the greatest show in Denver," or we'd always wonder.

There was a point in my life with God when, after I shed my dreams, I started viewing all my decisions that way. I'm not saying I always choose the crazy weird option. And I'm definitely not saying bad Mexican food is the story we're all going for. I'm just saying that when God became everything, from that point forward, I've always been aware that there is something bigger at play than what I am experiencing at that moment.

AT EVERY MOMENT OF THE JOURNEY—NOT JUST THE FORKS IN THE ROAD—THERE'S AN OPPORTUNITY, A CHOICE.

There's the chance to choose the normal, and there's a chance to choose a story. So often we don't even recognize that the choice is there.

As Heather and I sat there talking over biscuits with honey butter, I felt Ryan's little hand patting me on the arm. I turned to see what he needed, and he was totally engaged in a kids' show playing on Heather's iPad, earbuds in, right hand absently reaching out to pat me.

Heather laughed. "Oh, that one, he's affectionate," she said.

I reached out and patted the hand that was patting me and then tickled the arm attached to it, and he started laughing, a deep, genuine belly laugh. He'd done that at our Friendsgiving recently, a potluck that a bunch of us had right before Thanksgiving. He and one of the guys had started telling jokes, and he decided to make up one of his own.

"Who likes boogers?" he'd asked.

"Who?"

"The devil!" He started belly laughing so hard that he took everyone in the room down with him. You can't help but laugh back at that kind of joy-filled laugh.

This kid. We could've so easily missed out on knowing him. This sounds like the point where I say, "If Heather hadn't chosen to be a foster parent when she came to that fork in the road, we never would've known Ryan." But that wouldn't be accurate.

THE FACT IS, THERE WAS NO FORK IN THE ROAD. THIS WAS A STORY SHE WENT LOOKING FOR.

No one came to her and asked her to do it. She could've easily just kept doing her thing, living a pretty normal life, seeing if God brought along a husband one day, seeing if He brought her a different life.

But when she looked up and saw God for who He was, for all He was worth, she saw something else. She saw a thread dangling from the tapestry that He was weaving, a thread to a greater story. A thread that brought His love to people who needed it. A thread that touched a desire that He was growing in her heart to take care of others. A thread that wasn't meant to fulfill a selfish desire but to know more of God and His selfless love.

She couldn't see the whole story. She still can't. But that thread was enough. It was being held out to her by the God she loved and wanted to follow until she got home. It was a vital part of the bigger story. And she reached out and grabbed it.

God held out a thread like that to a guy named Abraham once. He saw God for who He was, and he fell on his face. And God said, "Walk before Me and be blameless, and I will be your God, and I will make you a part of a huge story that will impact generations and nations to come." In faith Abraham reached out and took hold of that thread.

He uprooted his family and followed God out into the great unknown, with nothing but the promise that God was going with him and that this was going to be a really great story. The kind we'll be talking about around the table in eternity.

Through him, God was going to call out a people for Himself, and from them would come Jesus, the One who would save us all from eternal suffering to a life with God face-to-face. God tested Abraham along the way. God asked him to give up the one thing most important to him. He asked him to follow Him indefinitely with no idea when the wandering would stop, or what he would encounter along the way.

Some of those tests Abraham passed with flying colors. Other times he made some poor decisions. I can relate to that. But ultimately Abraham's faithfulness in trusting God's promise and following Him outside of the life he had built for himself brought God's favor and blessing and a huge part in an eternal story. "For he was looking forward to the city that has foundations, whose designer and builder is God" (Hebrews 11:10). Now Abraham is seeing the fruit of his faith—he's face-to-face with the God who is his reward. And it wasn't just about him. He's seeing others join him as more and more people look up, see God through the gift of Christ, and take hold of that thread.

People like me. People like you. I'm not saying you have to go do something crazy or move overseas. You might need to do that. That might be the thread God is holding out to you. After all, we do all have that command. *Go and preach the gospel to all peoples.* But the point is that when we look to God, when we see Him for who He is—*the*

God who's bigger than the universe, the God of infinite love who runs to us, the God we can trust, the God who is worth everything—when He fills our heart up with Himself, we don't just sit there.

We love what He loves. We want what He wants.

WE ARE INTENTIONAL ABOUT FINDING WAYS TO BE A PART OF HIS BIG, BIG STORY.

And that big story involves us sharing that hope with those who don't have it.

That may mean we find a way to go live in a country where a lot of people don't know who our God is. That may mean we take in children who don't have families. That may mean we open our eyes to the internationals in our city and invite them into our homes and into our lives. That may mean that instead of choosing a new hobby for ourselves, we invest time and money in learning the language of a people who need to hear about His love.

All these options are messy, just like our relationship with God is messy. They may be uncomfortable. They may test us, exhaust us, stretch us. But the best stories never have been easy, and the whole thing is weaving something really, really amazing.

When the door opened to move to that other country, I'll admit I was surprised. That hadn't been part of the plan, and it wasn't on my radar.

BUT I COULD SEE THE THREAD THAT GOD HAD WOVEN THERE POKING OUT THROUGH THE MESS.

I knew that God had been laying the groundwork in my heart and life for a story involving that country ever since that first cup of coffee on a friend's couch in Birmingham.

And God's groundwork for my heart had started even before that, that day at 4:50 a.m. when I took a deep breath and told God I didn't want the old kind of normal.

I didn't know where to start. I didn't have a lot of time in the evenings. So the best way I could think of to get to know someone of another culture was to find a language tutor whom I could meet with weekly.

I found her number through the local culture center, and I picked up the phone and called her. It's not to my credit—I had no idea what I was doing. I was starting off down that unknown road just as blindly as Abraham walked out of his comfort zone.

But I had seen God before. And I knew I wanted momentum, momentum toward Him and His eternal story. Thankfully—just like with the guy who ended the relationship on the park bench, which in turn ended my England life sooner than I planned—God works in our decisions, big and small.

Because He is *in me*. He is *in us*.

HE DOESN'T WANT US TO AGONIZE OVER OUR CHOICES, BUT TO LIVE OUR LIVES, LIVING AND MOVING IN HIM.

So we turn our eyes up toward Him, toward that thread. We ask for eyes to see Him and to see the people around us, really see them. We invite them into our lives. We ask Him to help us love them like He does, even when we're tired, even when it's uncomfortable. He shines in our weakness, because He loves us, and He loves them.

Her hand patted me on the shoulder as we went over the last of the day's new vocabulary words. This friend—she was an affectionate one too. It was the last day of language tutoring in the country where I'd been hanging out temporarily. I'd spent month after month trying to learn to speak and read the language. I'd failed a whole lot. I'd laughed a whole lot. My friends there had laughed too. And before I knew it, the place felt a lot less foreign and a lot more like home.

Some things are the same no matter where you go. For women, this includes what we laugh at and what we think about. Occasionally, during our breaks at tutoring, my friend and I would split a pack of brownies, and from our window, she would pick out husbands for me on the street. Her local brand of speed dating taught me a lot of words. Like *rich*. And *ponytail*.

No surprise—I didn't find love there. But I did find something beautiful.

GOD BEGAN TO BLOSSOM SOMETHING HE HAD BEGUN MONTHS AND MONTHS AGO, AND IT WASN'T LONG BEFORE THIS PLACE AND ITS PEOPLE HAD WORKED THEIR WAY DEEP INTO MY HEART.

He grew a different kind of love in me that I believe hasn't seen the end of its plotline yet. He deepened the feeling in my soul that our lives are linear, that we're not meant for an earthly destination, not meant to sit, or to desire to achieve the place where we can.

We were meant to follow the thread until it gets us home, no matter what color it is, no matter whether it be dark or light, whether it leaves us in one place for a long, long while, or whether it keeps us on the move. All should be purposeful. All should be forward motion.

As I hugged my friend good-bye that day, tears welled

up in my eyes, and I told her I loved her. What she didn't realize is that in all of our conversations, all of our meals, she'd given me a gift far beyond what I could tell her. She'd been my friend. And she had been a big, big part of my tapestry, my story. And the thing is—we weren't even close to seeing the whole picture yet.

Sometimes I feel the tug of that particular thread in my heart, and I wonder where it's headed. I don't need to know, but I do need to follow. Even though we can't see the whole tapestry, once we start seeing the threads as purposeful parts of the story, we view our whole lives differently. We feel a forward pull. We feel the purpose of the present. We long for the overarching story.

Seeing things that way makes us ask different questions. It makes us give up smaller desires for bigger ones, bigger ones with infinite possibilities for fulfillment. Desires that can't be satiated over a pack of brownies.

Sometimes I think about the possibility of getting married, like that night I was lying there thinking about that engagement ring conversation I'd had with my friend. But even though I think about it, I think differently than I used to. I don't worry anymore that I'm missing out by not having a husband, or kids, or a certain life.

My heart asks different questions: *How many Ryans am I missing out on? How many people am I not seeing who live and work around me as I cruise through my day, through my life? How could I best use my time and resources not to wait on something, but to go somewhere? To help someone? To share hope with them?*

That shift in mind-set has nothing to do with me. It has everything to do with God. The truth is that I couldn't be weaker.

BUT PRAISE GOD WE HAVE A GOD WHO IS IN THE BUSINESS OF REDEEMING US AND OUR STORIES RIGHT WHERE WE ARE.

Praise God He redeems my story right where I am, and praise God He is changing my heart to love like His, to be like His more with every passing moment.

I fail. A lot. But I see His strength meet me there. As we work through it—my shortcomings, pain, frailty, self-ishness—I know Him better. I see His thread leading me a little more clearly.

Our choices don't have to be grandiose. But they do have to be God-centered. Our stories don't need to be ones for the headlines, but they do need to take us toward Him as fully and as fast as possible.

Choose to go. Choose to stay. Choose a thousand different things. But choose what you choose on *purpose*.

CHOOSE WHAT YOU CHOOSE FOR THE PURPOSE OF KNOWING HIM BETTER AND MAKING HIM KNOWN TO OTHER PEOPLE.

And don't wait. God said, "Walk before Me and be blameless, and I will be your God" (Genesis 17:1–2). Walk with Him. Reach out and grab the thread. And buckle up, because the story will just get richer, fuller from here. Because He is where the *best story is*.

AS YOU'VE CONTINUED TO GIVE MORE OF YOURSELF TO GOD AND LEARN MORE OF HIS WORD, HOW HAVE THE QUESTIONS YOU ASK ABOUT YOUR LIFE CHANGED?_____

_____

_____

_____

_____

_____

_____

_____

_____

_____

thirteen

WHY WE DON'T SETTLE

My lungs burned as we climbed the rocky path edging up the mountain toward St. Mary's Glacier. I stopped to breathe for a second, moving the camera strap I had slung across my chest, as if that would relieve the pressure. I turned to see how far we'd come. I could still see the parking lot. Right there. Right behind me.

They say you don't know what you've got until it's gone, and apparently I'd been living a life of decadent breathing at sea level, ignorantly indulging in the excess while my counterparts living at altitude were starving. I might as well have been going for a swim in Starbucks coffee thinking it was lake water.

I'd never realized I had such a luxury for free. Here in Colorado, it felt like my lungs were having to pluck individual specks of oxygen out of the sky and milk them for all they were worth. I felt like I needed a 152 sherpa. A yak. An oxygen tank. A minute.

"Take your time," Abi said, shifting back and forth on her feet as if she was ready to bound up the side of the mountain. Apparently, her hometown in New Mexico is at altitude too, so she was basically born ready for this.

While I collected myself, people were coming and going, casually walking their dogs. This little 10,000-foot-high mountain was easy pickings for the natives. I had friends from here who routinely climbed the state's 14ers—the 53 peaks that top 14,000 feet in elevation.

"Okay, let's go," I said finally as another small dog trotted by. "I'm fine."

We started again, and it did get easier, though I couldn't mask my wheezing. Eventually, we came to a clearing, and there she was. The first glacier I'd ever seen in real life.

St. Mary's Glacier cascaded down the side of the mountain, ice and snow glistening in the sun. It's as if it was caught off guard, frozen in motion on its way to the lake below. I can see why it would've been headed there. The lake was beautiful, a blue-green body of water set in between rocks and tall, rugged trees.

We sat. I could've stayed there all day. The trees wrapped around the scene, a bold green against the deepest blue sky I've ever seen. It was worth the walk, worth the labored breathing to get up there. I thought we might hang out for a while. I pulled out something to write on for a little bit.

"Nope, not yet," Abi said. "We still have to get up there." She pointed at the glacier.

I could see people moving around up there like ants. And before I could say anything, Abi was on the move again.

I put my stuff back together and followed her up the next leg of the rocky trail—even steeper than the one before. But no complaints from me. I wanted today to be the first day I ever made a snowball in weather hot enough for shorts and a T-shirt. So I walked on, and she was right. It was worth it.

From the top of the glacier, the Rockies stretched out on the horizon in layers—purple, green, and blue, and in the farthest distance sprinkled with snow at the crowns. The deep-blue lake mirrored the color of the sky and the trees around it. Below our feet, the glacier sat frozen in place, the bottom edge of it sloughing off into an icy mountain stream. The whole place was stunning. We sat in silence, taking in the view.

"You know what we almost did?" Abi said after a minute.

"What?"

"We almost settled for down there," she said, pointing to where we'd been sitting on the edge of the lake a few minutes ago.

"SURE, THAT WAS PRETTY. BUT WHY DO WE SETTLE SO MANY TIMES FOR DOWN THERE WHEN THERE'S ALL THIS UP HERE?"

The wind blew icy across the glacier in the beating sun, goose bumps rising on my arms. *Good question.*

That it's a question at all is crazy. Because when it comes to our lives, there's no reason to *ever* stay "down there," even on a human level. It's the same with our lives with God. There's no reason to ever choose *nice* over *amazing.* No one ever willingly chooses a gas station hamburger when a filet mignon sits on the same plate.

But the thing is—even though *nice* and *amazing* are equally attainable and free, in this scene they aren't necessarily on the same plate. God holds the free gift of *amazing* in outstretched hands to us every day. But though it's as free as *nice, amazing* does require a further climb—a determination to dig into His Word, His character, His love.

Sometimes we see that, and we just settle. It's the inclination of our sinful flesh. Somewhere between "down there" and "up here," something in the human DNA rises up and clogs the will to get us there, overrides our enthusiasm with lethargy, our determination with apathy. Suddenly, we all feel less than fully consumed with passion about it. We find ourselves having a big ol' dinner on the grounds "down there." The communal inertia doesn't help our case, for sure.

IT TAKES EFFORT TO CHOOSE NOT TO SETTLE. BUT IT'S INFINITELY WORTH IT.

Because for *the one who conquers* so they can sit "up here," there's the opportunity to sit smack in the middle of His love, His radiance. We can walk in it, enjoy it, touch it, pitch our tents in it. When we live in the reality of God's love, we feel His touch on each of us. On me. On you.

We feel His love for us even—and dare I say *especially*— in the way things didn't work out according to our plan. With His love sitting in our souls and writing our stories, we feel His affection *through* how our lives look, not *in spite* of it. We don't feel He's forgotten us; instead, we feel He's weaving our narratives with intentionality, taking the bad and turning it inside out, remaking us through pain in the redemptive way that only the loving God of the universe can do.

We pray for new, deep, eternity-sized dreams, and we see the way He moves in our lives as answers to those prayers. *God, I just want to know You better. Do whatever You need to do in my life for me to know You better.* Because of that prayer, and because of His love, we take the happy and the hard in equal stride. When the hard comes, the thought that bleeds from our hearts changes from *God, really? This is what You brought me?* to a very different sentiment: *This is the thing You've brought to accomplish Your purpose in my life. This isn't fun. This hurts. But please help me be a good steward of this. Help me know You better because of it.*

Though You slay me, yet I will praise You.

We ask Him to help us waste nothing because we know both the good and the bad carry eternal significance. With that in view, *all* of our moments become precious commodities. We don't stretch and strain to make everything serious every second, or push ourselves to burnout. But we *do* feel the glorious weight of how each moment is part of a greater whole, and we feel *lighter* because of that, not heavier. We aim not to waste a drop because we become aware that each minute is golden, a chance to live in the reality of His love, a chance to worship, to spend our lives doing what we were designed to do—to walk in the joy of worshipping the One who loved us first.

And that's how we get to see the best plot twists happen, the ones written for our specific frame and personality, our time and place in history, and the square foot of space we're standing on at any given moment. That's how we see our teeny, tiny vapor of a life click into place in the grand, overarching story that God is writing over the span of eternity.

That's how the best narratives happen. Yours. Mine.

I don't need my story to look fancy. I don't need it to look traditional, and I don't need it to be crazy and adrenaline filled. *I just need it to give me more of Jesus.* I don't want to settle for anything less.

There's a lot of clarity that comes from sitting on top of mountains. I think that's one reason I used to love to sit on that big green hill in England and watch the tiny, Dairy Queen-size trains go by in the valley.

SITTING UP HIGH HAS A WAY OF BRINGING PERSPECTIVE. IT REMINDS US OF HOW SMALL THE SMALL THINGS ARE, AND HOW BIG THE BIG THINGS ARE.

It's a place where heaven touches earth, where mercy meets humanity. And I love it. I love how when we sit there, things below become quiet and we feel it über-strongly— the upward pull, the desire for our stories to resolve and find their apex. We weren't made to want mundane.

WE WERE MADE TO WANT MORE. AND THERE'S A REASON FOR THAT.

There is more to be had. Everything in us screams for more. Our hearts long for it. That's why we do what we do. That's why we dream what we dream. We want real love, so we spend our lives looking for it. We want real purpose, so we spend our lives trying to get it. *And if we never look up, we never find it.* From an earthly perspective, it almost seems like a cruel device hardwired into our hearts—the yearning that can never be satisfied. But God didn't miss a step when He built us lacking, built us to crave.

HE WANTED US TO LOOK FOR HIM UNTIL WE FOUND HIM. HE WANTED OUR HEARTS FOR HIMSELF.

What a story. What an incredible, impossible story.

Seriously, why would a God who can speak the world into existence write something like this and let us be a part of it? *What an amazing Maker.*

From up here on the mountain above all the small stuff, it's clear. We can see it. We see God for who He is. A treasure worth everything. We see that the story that gets us to Him is *so much greater* than the dreams we had for ourselves that didn't work out. We see that the things we *do* have here are gifts we put toward God's story, things that are meant to keep us in forward motion, eyes fixed on eternity. We see that this whole thing we're a part of here is bigger than spending our time mourning our broken dreams. We see that even the deepest pain is preparing us for the place where we will find infinite comfort and unlimited joy.

And we see that the God of the universe is within our reach, if we'll choose not to settle for the good things here that betray the great things there.

We choose Him. We choose to give Him everything. Again and again and again. Daily. We choose not to wait anymore. And we walk on, hearts full, eyes locked on eternity.

As a writer, I get really excited about endings. I love it when they're well written. I love a good story that gets us to that moment of resolution with hearts pounding, souls bursting. It's a shame that for a while there I let the best ending of all get buried in a muddled mess of misunderstanding in my heart.

It's the ending God has written for those who love Him, for those to whom He said, "Follow Me," and they threw off houses and land and possessions and dreams and followed Him. For the ones who didn't settle, who in His strength kept moving forward and conquered what tried to weigh them down on earth.

That view from St. Mary's Glacier makes my heart

think of that ending, though it doesn't touch what it will actually look like—the scene that one day will pierce our souls with its beauty, the place where our yearnings will find rest. It's at the banks of the river of life, bright as crystal, from which we as His children can drink for free—because Christ bought that life for us. Where there will be no pain, no night, only light and joy and God. Forever.

The Bible paints us a picture of what it's going to look like when we see God, and it is stunning. It's also, surprisingly, in the last place we look, or care to look. The last few pages of Revelation. I'll admit, for years I avoided that book. It was all kinds of scary. It made me nervous, all those hard-to-decode descriptions of boils and horsemen and dragons. What Starbucks-drinking, 8-to-5 normal American wants to sit down on a regular basis and seriously consider that his or her life might end in beasts and beheadings and antichrists? I'd venture to say not many. I know I sure didn't.

I remember going to a youth conference in the eighth grade that was all about the signs of the end times and how we could know when the rapture was coming. The cover of the workbook had a picture of somebody's legs and shoes flying into the air. If that's not hard to relate to as a Mississippi middle schooler, I don't know what is.

At one point after we'd all been scared silly, and the entire auditorium had joined hands to sing a song about walking down the road toward eternity together, there was a thunderclap outside, and thousands of teenagers all freaked out simultaneously because we thought God was coming back to take us all. It was hilarious. And it was scary stuff. As a teen, the thought of my shoes being propelled from earth as I shot through the air to meet God was almost as scary as the dragons and beasts and antichrists. I don't think I was alone in that.

If the screams all over that auditorium weren't enough to prove it, the other day I asked my friend Lauren—who was also at that conference—if she remembered if she had any fond feelings toward Revelation at that age, or if she thought about it at all.

"Very little," she said. "I think I tried not to because I knew I didn't want it to happen."

I think I carried that same impression with me for a long, long time—into adulthood. I didn't want it to happen. I wanted nothing in that book to happen. It kept me up at night. All the seemingly crazy junk drowned out anything good that might've been there, and even if I heard the good, I didn't know God well enough for Him to feel like a refuge in the middle of the ultimate scare tactic of the book that was Revelation.

And therein was the key. *I didn't know God well enough. I hadn't made that climb.*

Not until much, much later did someone show me what

that book was really meant to be about, and everything changed. My feelings did a one-eighty, turning the book I avoided like the plague into the story I loved the most. It all comes down to the last few pages. Ultimate hope is buried right there behind all that hard-to-read stuff. Except it wasn't meant to be buried.

THAT HOPE WAS MEANT TO BE THE APEX THAT OUR HEARTS ARE YEARNING FOR.

My pastor in Alabama said once that Revelation was never meant for us to figure out exactly how God was going to play everything out. All that stuff in John's vision of the end times is important, and we definitely get the picture well enough that nothing with its roots in the earth is going to end well. But that book was written with a different purpose in mind—to give hope to the hurting. It was written to the believers, the ones who were facing hard times, pain, opposition, and persecution, so that they would know that no matter how bad things got, "the one who conquers will have this heritage, and I will be his God and he will be my son" (Revelation 21:7). It was to say, "Fix your eyes on this." They did. *And so should we.*

Week after week at my church in Alabama, as we took the bread and the cup together, our pastor would say, "We do this in anticipation of the day that we will drink this cup together with Christ in His kingdom."

Because we will. We will drink it there with Jesus. And when we do, the yearning in our hearts will dissipate for good. We'll have everything our souls ever wanted, fulfillment infinitely better than anything we could've settled for here on earth. *And that is the best ending any of us could ever dream of.*

The tiny cup in my hand turned blurry in an instant. But things had never been clearer. I sat there, tears spilling from my eyes, the red contents of the cup stirring as I turned it in my fingers. *This is it. Right here.*

The best stories are always in the future in the kingdom of God.

The words the Denver pastor had said just moments before were still ringing in my ears. This cup that I squeezed between my fingers—one day soon I would be drinking this *with Christ.* In a place where there's no pain, only joy; no darkness, only light. How can that fact ever get stale? How is it possible that I willingly stop short of the highest joy, the highest peace, when it's in view? Why do I settle for good things here that are barely a shadow of the things to come? The joy of His kingdom still to come really can make our cups overflow here as this becomes a wispy, temporary chapter barely capable of introducing the grand, unending story. *The best stories are always in the future in the kingdom of God.* I drank the cup dry.

After the service, Abi took my car keys from me. She saw the tears. She figured it was better if she drove and I talked.

"So . . . what's going on in there, Grace?" she asked, waving her hand in the direction of my head.

It was hard to sum up what was going on "in there," the mountains, cups, rivers of crystal, trees of life all swirling around. I'm a lover of stories. I think the best ones are the ones God gives us. And I also believe the best are yet to come.

"I was reminded this morning that it's going to be okay," I said. "That God has this story written already. That it may be hard, but it ends really, really well. And that I feel most like myself, most alive, when the joy of what's still to come in Christ fills me up, when I'm overflowing with it." *I feel most like myself, most alive, because of Christ. Because of the life yet to come in Him.*

It had been a long journey to get to that realization. It had taken the death of my plans to reveal the cavernous longing in my heart, a longing that could never be satisfied by the things of this world. And it had taken seeing that a real, universe-size love existed before I saw I'd been settling for a weak, faded love that barely put a dent in my longing.

Praise God.

PRAISE GOD FOR THAT BIG LOVE THAT BURSTS OUR SOULS.

Praise Him for the fact that He saw fit to come down, pursue my heart, and die in my place. And praise Him for the people who have that reality oozing out of their eyeballs so that people like me can see that *it's real, that it's not just words, and that it wrecks you from the inside out . . . forever. For the better.*

Because of that light on the horizon, that light in people's eyes, I pushed into His Word, plunging my face into it, airing out the dusty corners of my heart. He met me there. He moved from my pocket and into my heart. He held out His arms, and I threw off my heavy plans and hurts and dreams and I jumped. He became my everything.

He began to spin a story greater than anything I had ever seen, more meaningful than anything I could've dreamed, with threads woven into them that the greatest storyteller on earth could never come up with in a million years.

AND THE BEST PART IS . . . THE TOP SIDE OF THE TAPESTRY HAS YET TO BE SEEN.

It was the idea of the unseen picture that was circling in my head that day in the car with Abi, the apex of the story my soul's been longing for, the one whose weight I feel but whose complete picture I had yet to see. The One who is everything we could ever want, for all eternity. My soul, my eyes overflowed.

Never settle, Grace. Never settle for worry or anxiety, for doubt or discontent, for distrust or frustration when ultimate joy is there for the taking. Here today. And even greater still to come.

BE HONEST: WHAT IS KEEPING YOU FROM ASKING GOD FOR THE STORY THAT MOVES YOU CLOSER TO HIM—AND FROM WANTING IT MORE THAN ANYTHING ELSE? ARE YOU WILLING TO LET GO OF ANYTHING HOLDING YOU BACK?

_____

_____

_____

_____

_____

_____

_____

_____

_____

SERIOUSLY, THOUGH—HOW DO I DO THIS?

When my friend Clare saw God for who He really is and came to believe in Him, she did an all-in, go-for-broke, cannonball-off-the-cliff kind of plunge into the freedom of His love. But I didn't do it that way. I believed, I grew, but real freedom came way later. Years. Almost decades. For all of us, the journey looks different.

Hero of the faith George Mueller described his life with God in two parts—the first several years he knew God, and then the moment when everything changed drastically. He called it the "full surrender of the heart." When that happened, Mueller said, "The love of money was gone, the love of place was gone, the love of position was gone, the love of worldly pleasures and engagements was gone. God, God, God alone became my portion. I found my all in Him; I wanted nothing else. And by the grace of God this has remained, and has made me a happy man, an exceedingly happy man, and it led me to care only about the things of God." His heart became so full in that season that it made him wonder if he'd ever really known God before.

The catalyst that led to that point? *Plunging headlong into Scripture and really seeing who God is.* "I read a little of the Scriptures before," he said, "but preferred other books, but since that time the revelation He has made of Himself [in the Bible] has become unspeakably blessed to me."

God's love reaches out for your heart from the pages of His Word, just like it did for George Mueller. It takes effort and discipline to reach back and dig in. But there are no DIY steps because we're getting to know an infinite God, not a guidebook.

The only step is to come to the Word with open hands and a heart of desire, and from there God begins to rewrite our miniscule view of Him into something grandiose. Revelation enlarges our hearts for God, shaves off the burden of the worldly things we dream of. The more we drop, the higher we can hold our empty hands.

It's messy, friends. But He's worth it. He's worth committing to in order to figure it out for yourself, whatever it takes. So—seriously. How do we do this? The type of raw prayers I've prayed, the Scriptures that have seared themselves in my heart through reading and meditation—those are laced through this book just like they're laced through my story.

Here are a few practices that have helped me along the

way, just in case they help you too. They're not a formula, but a place you can start to do this on your own.

- → Spend time with God. There's no way around this one. We're busy people, some of us with families and crazy jobs and other obligations, and God honors our faithfulness in giving what we have to give. But if He doesn't get the lion's share of my heart and time, and things like sleep and television and Facebook do, I can't expect Him to become large in my heart. The things here will.

- → Find your own rhythm. We all have to find a personal rhythm that works for us. It's not about legalism, but it *is* about discipline—we care enough to set aside the time and the effort to get to know the God of the universe. It can be morning, afternoon, night, some of the above, all of the above. But the more, the better.

- → Read. Read lots. And then read some more. If you've never really read the Bible much before, the book of John is a good place to start. It tells the story of how God became flesh in Jesus and lived among us here so that we could know Him better. That's some goodness for your soul to digest, and a great place to start.

→ When we go to God's Word, it's important that we put on the right lens. It's vital that we read from the perspective that we're going to learn more about who God is, not read a guidebook to our lives. It was always meant to be about God, not about us. But learning who He is—and learning what His love looks like—changes everything about us.

→ You don't have to be a historian or a theologian or a member of the clergy to read the Bible and understand it—the words are living and active, and the Holy Spirit helps us understand them as we read and study. But we need to know the context of the stories and the advice being shared—why God did what He did at that time and place and why He said what He said to those people in that specific place and time.

→ If you have a study Bible, it may have an introduction to each book that explains why the book was written and to whom it was written. Understanding this is key—God had a specific meaning in mind for each verse the Bible contains. We don't read with the lens of "What does this verse mean to me?"—it wasn't written for us to apply to our lives like the words of a fortune cookie. We read with the lens of "God, help me understand and know You better." And as we know Him, He changes our hearts and we hear His voice. And freedom happens.

→ Ask God to show you the truth of who He is as you read. It's you and Him. Just talk to Him. Read about Him. Study His words. Get to know Him. The Holy Spirit, our Teacher, meets you there.

→ Find a structure that works for you. There are methods and plans and all kinds of help out there to provide structure for Bible reading, if you want or need it. Some people use reading plans that tell them what to read every day. Some of those plans read straight through the Bible from front to back. Some read a little in the Old Testament (the first part of the Bible, which tells the story of God's people before Jesus came) and the New Testament (the second part, which tells the story of Jesus' coming) each day. Some read a passage from Psalms and Proverbs every day.

→ For me, the thing that's been most effective is a plan that has me reading in several different places in the Bible at one time, with a little bookmark for each section. That may sound intimidating, but I like it because it isn't dated or divided by daily readings. If I want to read something from all of the sections, I can, or if I want to only read one and really meditate on it and pray over it for a long time that day, I can. That way I'm always moving forward but never falling behind, and I never feel like I have to frantically catch up. I have time to take a deep breath and really sit with one passage if it feels like that's what God is leading me to do that morning. I can pray over it. I can read it out loud.

➤ With that kind of plan, I feel disciplined but not legalistic, and that works for me. Something else might work really well for you. Just try a few options—I've put a few under the How to Know God More tab at gracefortheroad.com if you'd like a place to start. See what happens. Just whatever you do, stick with it.

➤ Let the Word soak in. Give yourself the time and space to read a passage, reread it verse by verse, let the words soak into your mind and heart. Let the truth wash over you in a way that it sticks. Memorize verses and passages that speak needed truth to your soul. Make sticky notes. Write it on your mirror. Whatever it takes for you to write it on your heart, because that's when it will begin to change your life.

→ Journal, if you like. When I read, I also journal, which works really well for me—but I know not everyone loves journaling. I write what God is teaching me, I write verses that jump out at me, and sometimes I write out my prayers, though my favorite way is to say them out loud, just talking with God as though He's in the room with me. (He is.) Sometimes I listen to worship music, and I draw pictures in my journal of the things I learn and love about God. I'm not artistic, but it helps me meditate on those things and gives me visuals to remember who He is.

→ Talk with others. Connect with a local, small group that values studying the Bible together too—that's a great way to learn from what others are doing and learning. Even though our relationship with God is really personal, it was also meant to be lived in community. In talking about what God's teaching us in His Word, we sharpen each other.

So that's enough from me—it's time for me to leave you to start working out what pursuing God looks like in your life. I'd love to hear what you're learning—come drop me a line at gracefortheroad.com. Remember, that climb to breathe free takes time. But He's worth it. He's worth it all—our time, our discipline, our dreams, our lives.

Run His way. Run hard. And for the love, don't ever stop.